THE INTERNET

MARY LOJKINE

In easy steps is an imprint of Computer Step
Southfield Road . Southam
Warwickshire CV47 0FB . United Kingdom
www.ineasysteps.com

Notice of Liability
Every effort has been made to ensure that this book contains
accurate and current information. However, Computer Step and the
author shall not be liable for any loss or damage suffered by readers
as a result of any information contained herein.

Trademarks
All trademarks are acknowledged as belonging to their respective
companies.

The right of Mary Lojkine to be identified with this work has been
asserted by her in accordance with the Copyright, Designs and
Patents Act 1988.

Printed and bound in the United Kingdom

ISBN-13: 978-1-84078-285-1
ISBN-10: 1-84078-285-4

Table of Contents

Lost and found

4

Lights, camera, cue music, action 71

5

It's a rich man's world 93

6

Fancy filework 105

7

Questions, questions...

You've heard of the Internet, of course – there can't be many people who haven't. But what is it, exactly? Where did it come from, how does it work and, most importantly, what good is it? This chapter provides the answers.

Covers

Chapter One

Hello...

...and welcome to the Internet. Put your coat over there, grab a drink from the bar and join the party!

To be honest, you're a little late. The invites went out in the mid 1990s, the DJ arrived in 1997 and the Internet has been a big, wild, rock 'n' roll extravaganza ever since. Still, you're here now... and it isn't such a bad time to arrive. The party is settling down and all the guests are getting mellow. The neighbors have been round to complain about the noise and now they're sat over there with a glass of wine, making friends. No more worries on that front. There was an awkward moment when the venture capitalists got upset about the money they'd spilt, but we've mopped everything up and you can hardly see the stain. We've sorted out the problem with the sound system, we've sent someone out for more beer, and the pizzas will be arriving any minute. In short, it's a better party than it was five years ago.

Making the most of the Internet used to require technical know-how, blind faith, a fat wallet and a fair degree of patience. In 2005 you don't need any of those things. It's easy to get connected and it costs very little. The Internet has become more versatile, too. You can access all sorts of information, from today's news to descriptions of the plumbing systems in ancient Egypt, and do all sorts of useful things. You can communicate with your friends, shop for a new home and everything that goes in it, pay your bills, find phone numbers, look up addresses on an interactive map, book your holidays and even file your tax return. The Internet has become an important part of day-to-day life.

This book will drag you on to the Internet, kicking and screaming, and show you all its best features (the kicking and screaming is optional, okay?). You'll learn how to choose a modem, find an Internet service provider, make a connection, browse the Web, dispatch an email, participate in a newsgroup, send an instant message and create a Web page. For starters, though, you might be wondering what the Internet is, where it came from and how it works. This chapter answers all those questions.

Grab a seat, help yourself to pretzels and read on...

What is the Internet?

The Internet is the hottest thing since boy bands, the coolest thing since flares and the best thing since sliced bread. It's in the news, it's on TV, it has a bit part in your favorite soap operas. Your children are using it at school, your coworkers swear by it (or at it) and your elderly grandmother keeps asking you how it works. If you haven't heard of the Internet, you must have been living on a mountain, in a far-off country, for the last ten years.

But what is it, exactly?

The Internet (or Net) is a computer network that spans the globe. It consists of millions of computers that are physically connected, using wires and cables and satellite connections, so information can pass from one computer to the next.

You might have heard people talking about the "information superhighway". In reality, the Internet is more like the entire road network, from the smallest country road to the largest highway, along with all the ferries that let you take your car across the sea. Just as the road network lets you drive to any house or building that's actually on a road, the Internet lets you send information to any computer that's connected to the network. Computers that aren't connected are like caves on faraway mountains – the information that's on them, like the people who live in the caves, has no contact with the outside world.

The difference between the Internet and the road network is that information flies from computer to computer at speeds motorists can only dream of. Although it's technically possible to drive from Boston, Massachusetts, in the United States to Boston, Free State, in South Africa (with the help of ferries), it would take you weeks. On the Internet, data moves so quickly that the distance between computers is irrelevant. It doesn't matter whether the information you need is stored on a computer in your home town, or on a computer on the other side of the world. Either way, it reaches your computer in seconds.

So that's all there is to it?

Not exactly. Computers and cables are only half the story. To do anything productive with the Internet, you also need software to manage the information and move it about. Otherwise it's just going to sit on a computer, taking up space.

People have all kinds of information they want to share, including facts, figures, stories, pictures, sounds and programs, and all kinds of ways to share it. Some information is private and needs to go to a specific person. Some can be made available to everyone. Some things are only relevant for a short period and must be transmitted quickly. Others may be useful for years to come. If you're inviting a friend to meet you for lunch, you don't want to immortalize your plans in a public forum. The restaurant, on the other hand, might want to advertize its menu to everyone, 24/7.

There are many different ways to send information over the Internet. Each method has its own software and procedures. This book deals with four common ways to use the Internet:

- **The World Wide Web (or Web)** consists of millions of magazine-style pages packed with text, pictures, sounds, animations and video clips. They are linked together by electronic cross-references that enable you to jump from page to page. Information on the Web can be accessed by anyone, so it's used for news, reference material, information about products and events, and entertainment. You'll learn more about the Web and the software it requires – a Web browser – in Chapters 3, 4, 5, 6 and 7. Chapter 12 explains how to create your own Web pages.

Get the latest news from CNN's Web site, at: http:// www.cnn.com/

- **Electronic mail (or email)** is the Internet equivalent of letters and faxes. It enables you to send private messages to other Internet users, almost instantaneously. You can also send documents and pictures with your messages. Email and email programs are covered in Chapters 8 and 9.

Email is ideal
for quick notes

- **Usenet newsgroups** are public discussion forums where people exchange gossip, trivia, advice, insults and – very occasionally – news. They're the Internet equivalent of your local bar or social club, although there's no beer (alas). Newsgroups are accessed with a newsreader and are covered in Chapter 10.

- **Instant messaging (or chat)** enables you to conduct live, real-time conversations with other Internet users. You type instead of talking, but otherwise it's like gossiping on the phone. Some instant-messaging programs let you hook up a microphone and/or video camera and converse with sound and/or pictures. Instant messaging is covered in Chapter 11.

There are other ways to use the Internet and no doubt there'll be many more applications in the future. Remember that the Internet provides the infrastructure and the software makes things happen. To return to the road analogy, once the road network reaches your front door, you can take off on a bicycle or a motorbike, or in a car or a bus or a truck, depending on your destination and the amount of gear you need to carry.

Where did it come from?

The Internet turned 30 a few years ago (really, it's that old). Like any 30-something, it has some quirky habits born of its childhood experiences, so it's worth knowing how it evolved.

The Cold War

Back in the days when nuclear holocaust seemed imminent, the US Government decided to connect up some of its computers so scientists and military agencies could communicate more easily. Instead of building a single control center, which an enemy might destroy, the designers created a system where each computer operated independently. Messages traveled by any available route, rather than in fixed patterns. Even if some of the computers were destroyed by a military or terrorist attack, the others could carry on working. The first messages were transmitted in 1969.

The legacy of this period is a robust network that isn't disrupted by computer crashes and power cuts.

The nerd days

In the 1970s several more computer networks were established by military and academic institutions. Eventually they were joined together, creating a network of networks or "Internetwork". It was like the building of the Channel Tunnel between the United Kingdom and France: there were arguments about which side of the wires the messages should travel on, but eventually everyone agreed on common standards for transferring information.

This period gave us the term "Internet". It was also a time when computers were used primarily by scientists, academics and students (nerds and geeks, basically), so many of the developments were inspired by the desire to discuss *Star Trek* and tell bad jokes.

The age of the Internet

For more about the man who invented the Web, Tim Berners-Lee, visit his Web site, at: http://www.w3.org/People/Berners-Lee/

Everything changed in the 1990s, when the World Wide Web was developed by a British scientist working in Switzerland. Suddenly the Internet was attractive and easy to use, and you didn't need a degree in computer science to see the point. New software was developed by mainstream companies and distributed in cereal boxes (practically). Many more people had access to computers. Millions of them got connected. And people like you started buying books like this.

How does it work?

If you'd like to know more about internal combustion engines and cathode ray tubes, visit the HowStuffWorks Web site, at: http://www.howstuffworks.com/

Do you know how the engine in your car works? Or how the cathode ray tube in your television puts a picture on the screen? No? You don't need to know how the Internet works, either, but it's kind of interesting (if you disagree, you can skip this section).

Where's your computer?

Just as your house has a unique postal address, every computer on the Internet has a unique numeric address called an IP number. It consists of four numbers, separated by dots (periods). For example, 64.236.24.28 is the address of the computer that stores CNN's Web site.

IP is short for Internet Protocol, a set of rules for making up addresses and moving information around the Internet.

I can't remember that!

Numeric addresses are fine for computers, but human beings are better at remembering words. All the important computers on the Internet also have user-friendly names, such as www.cnn.com The Domain Name System (DNS) converts these names into numbers when a computer needs to find something.

*Once you've learned how to use a Web browser (Chapter 3), you can test this system. Run your browser and type **64.236.24.28** into the Address bar. You should end up at CNN's Web site.*

DNS is like a giant phone book for the Internet. When you ask your computer to fetch information from www.cnn.com, it contacts one of the computers that hold the DNS database, looks up the name, finds out that you're talking about the computer at 64.236.24.28, and then contacts that machine.

Let's get moving

You don't want to transmit information in big chunks, because if something goes wrong (such as the military attack the original designers feared), you'll lose everything. It's better to divide the information into small pieces, dispatch the pieces separately, and then reassemble them at the other end.

There's another set of rules for this procedure. Transmission Control Protocol (TCP) explains how to break up a lump of computer data into small "packets" and add the destination to each one, along with the address of the computer that's sending the data. The packets can then be transferred across the Internet, following the rules laid down by Internet Protocol. When they get to the other end, Transmission Control Protocol takes over again, checks that all the packets are present and reassembles them.

This system is very flexible. If there's a problem somewhere along the way, the packets are rerouted to avoid it. They might not all take the same route, and some packets go missing and have to be sent again, but everything gets there in the end. Also, information flows smoothly, because different people's packets can be mixed together. No-one gets to monopolize the wires.

Fun for everyone

The other good thing about this system is that the two important protocols, TCP and IP, can be implemented on almost any computer. Once your computer is physically connected to the Internet (more on that on page 16), you run a small program that creates a TCP/IP interface. This software is usually built in to your operating system (it is part of Windows, for example). It runs automatically when you try to use the Internet.

The TCP/IP software differs from computer to computer, but the rules are the same for everyone. It doesn't matter whether you use a PC or an Apple Mac to connect to the Internet, because both computers use the same procedures when they're sending and receiving information. You can think of TCP and IP as a set of road rules that everyone follows, no matter what type of computer they drive. The difference is that on the Internet, people actually follow the rules! If they don't, their data doesn't go anywhere.

The bottom line

You don't need to remember any of this and there certainly won't be a test, but since you've read this far, here's the cheat sheet:

- Each computer on the Internet has a unique address.

- When you transmit data, your computer uses Transmission Control Protocol (TCP) to divide it into small packets.

- Internet Protocol (IP) shifts the packets across the Internet, by any convenient route. TCP reassembles them.

- Any computer that can "do" TCP/IP can connect to the Net.

Who's in charge?

People used to believe that no-one owned or controlled the Internet. It was the Wild West of computing, a lawless frontier where anyone could set up camp and behave as they pleased. Sadly, the truth isn't quite as exciting.

Mine, mine, all mine...

The physical infrastructure of the Internet didn't just spring out of the ground. Every computer, every cable, every wire and every switch belongs to someone. In the early days, most of the hardware was owned by public institutions such as universities. Now much of it is installed and operated on a commercial basis. If a company wants to pull the plug on its computer, it can... but there are so many computers out there that you won't notice the difference. No-one owns enough of the Internet to seize control.

...and you'll do as you're told

All sorts of people have a say in how you use the Internet:

- To get connected, you'll need to sign up with an Internet service provider (see overleaf). You give the company money, it gives you access. As in any other commercial relationship, you're bound by the terms of the contract. If you break the rules, you'll be shown the door.

- There are several organizations that set standards and keep everything working. The Internet Society (ISOC) oversees the development of the Internet. Organizations under its control include the Internet Engineering Task Force (IETF), which deals with technical problems. The Internet Corporation for Assigned Names and Numbers (ICANN) keeps the address book in order and the World Wide Web Consortium (W3C) takes care of the Web.

- Governments are increasingly aware of the Internet. Sometimes they create new laws to deal with it, but often the existing legislation is sufficient. You can't (legally) make threats, libel people, steal copyrighted material or view hard-core pornography on the Internet, any more than you can in real life.

Of course, if you have a complaint about the Internet, no-one is going to admit to being responsible for even the smallest part of it!

How do I join?

You'll find out how to connect to the Internet in Chapter 2. For now, here's a quick overview.

You need four things to join the Internet:

- **A computer.** The simplest option is to use a PC running Windows. You can also use an Apple Mac or, if you're looking for a challenge, almost any computer ever invented.

- **A physical connection** between your computer and the Internet. In a perfect world, there'd be Internet cables running down your street, alongside the power lines and phone cables and water pipes. However there aren't many towns with hot and cold running Internet (yet), so you'll probably make a temporary connection using a modem – a device that enables computers to communicate with each other via a telephone line. Information travels from your computer to the modem, which sends it down the phone line to another modem, which is attached to another computer, which belongs to…

- **An Internet service provider (ISP).** Internet service providers make it possible for ordinary people to access the Internet from their back bedrooms. They have computers that are permanently wired up to the Internet, and also to banks of modems. Once you've opened an account, you use your modem to make a connection to one of your ISP's modems, and thence to the Internet. Service providers also take care of housekeeping tasks such as storing and forwarding your electronic mail.

- **Internet software.** As you learned earlier, a physical connection is only half the story. To do anything useful, you'll need computer programs that enable you to send and receive information. Most new computers come with everything you'll need. If you have an older model, you can get software from your service provider, from the CDs attached to computer magazines, or from computer shops.

That's all there is to it: computer, modem, ISP, software… Internet.

HOT TIP

You can also use a special modem that connects your computer to the cable television network – see page 28 for more details.

Why should I bother?

There are many, many reasons why you should drop everything (except this book) and get connected to the Internet:

- **To stay in touch.** It isn't the multimedia glory of the Web that attracts most people, but the practicality of electronic mail. Whether you're communicating with colleagues in the next office or friends on the other side of the world, email is quick, cheap and convenient. Whereas a letter might take a few days to arrive, an email message takes a few seconds – and it costs less to send. And unlike a phone call, it'll never disrupt an important meeting or wake someone up.

- **To meet people.** With over 900 million people using the Net, there are bound to be a few who share your interests. You can find people who want to chat about anything from ancient Greek to football – be it American football, English football (also known as soccer) or Aussie Rules – to your favorite television show. Is he cheating on her? Will she keep the baby? There are people who care.

- **It's useful.** Want to know whether it's going to rain? Look out the window. Want to know whether it's going to rain in Spain, next week, when you're there on holiday? Find a forecast on the Internet. You can look up phone numbers, find a map of your neighborhood, check your bank balance, pay your bills, order flowers for your mother's birthday, see what movies are showing and find out which bus to catch.

Get worldwide weather forecasts from the Weather Channel's site, at: http://www.weather.com/ or order flowers from 1-800-flowers.com, at: http://www.800flowers.com/

- **It's fun.** The Web isn't just the world's largest magazine, it's also an enormous electronic toy box. There are stories to read, pictures to view, movie trailers to watch, sports highlights to relive and games to play. And every joke ever told is out there somewhere, waiting to be told again.

Watch cartoons and play games, at: http://www. shockwave.com/ or enjoy the strangeness of Monty Python, at: http://www.pythonline.com/

- **It's convenient.** Unlike a public library, the Internet is open 24 hours a day, seven days a week, throughout the year. You don't have to waste time traveling or finding a car park, and when you come across useful information, you don't have to queue for the photocopier – you just print it out.

- **It's up to date.** Libraries only have the facts that have been around long enough to make it into books. The Internet has the very latest information, including news too new for this morning's paper. And thanks to the power of electronic indexing, it's easy to find the stories you want to read, no matter when they were published. You can flip back to older bulletins and follow a story from its roots.

- **It does the math.** There are currency convertors that not only give you the exchange rate, but also work out how many Guatemalan Quetzels you'll get for your 23 Honduran Lempira. In some countries you can do your taxes on the Internet and have your bill calculated automatically.

- **It resolves arguments.** Can't remember who said golf was "a good walk spoiled"? Ask the Internet! What's the shortest English word that contains all five vowels, in order? Ask the Internet! All those snippets of information that have slipped down behind the cushions in your brain are waiting to be rediscovered, whenever you get the urge.

- **To promote your business.** The more people rely on the Internet for information, the more important it is to create a Web site for your business. Without a virtual shop-front in the Internet mall, you're invisible to millions of customers.

Find out more about the "in easy steps" range from the Computer Step Web site, at: http://www.ineasysteps.com/ or go scuba diving with Singapore-based Marsden Bros, at: http://www.marsbros.com/

- **To save money.** It costs almost nothing to send an email. You can stop buying newspapers and magazines. Internet shops offer better prices than real-world stores, because their costs are lower. You can download free or cheap software instead of paying for almost-empty shrink-wrapped boxes.

- **To make the most of your computer.** You probably spent a large sum of money on that large lump of beige plastic. It isn't decorative, so you might as well make it useful.

- **It's the future.** When Gutenberg invented the printing press, people probably told him reading was just for monks. In today's world of newspapers, novels, textbooks, bus timetables and warning signs telling you to "mind the gap", not being able to read is an enormous handicap. In the not-too-distant future, it'll be the same with the Internet. Enormous amounts of information are being moved on to the Web and hundreds of services are being computerized. You'll need to know your mouse from your menu.

But what about…

…the things that go bump in the night? What about the porn merchants peddling dirty pictures, the nasty viruses, the men pretending to be women, the thieves stealing credit-card numbers, the pedophiles preying on small children and the hackers trying to bring down the whole system? What if it all goes horribly wrong?

Truthfully, the Internet does have some dark, nasty corners, just as many towns have areas that are best avoided in the early hours of the morning. However, if you educate yourself about the problems, a night out on the Net won't leave you with a headache.

If you have children, you're probably concerned about them encountering adult material – or the wrong kind of adult. The best solution is to make Web browsing a family affair. Keep the computer in the living room so you can see what's on the screen.

Teach your children not to give out personal details, such as their full name or your address and phone number, and make sure they understand that people aren't always who they seem to be. If your children are too young to be wary of strangers, they're too young to use the Internet unsupervised.

To avoid computer viruses, start by learning how to recognize a potential threat (try turning to pages 111 and 138). Install antivirus software and update it regularly. To be completely safe, make back-up copies of files that contain important information or would be difficult to replace.

Online shopping is safer than you think, for two reasons. First, credit card fraud is more of a problem for retailers than it is for consumers, because the retailers foot the bill (check your terms and conditions, though). Second, there are many ways of stealing credit card numbers that require much less skill than intercepting Internet transactions. Chapter 6 explains the things to watch out for when you buy things over the Internet.

Hackers go after the rich and famous, which – no offence intended – probably doesn't mean you. If your computer contains valuable or confidential information, such as medical records or military schematics, you should take extra precautions when you connect it to the Internet (and don't leave it in a taxi). If you're Joe Ordinary, you have less to worry about. See page 113 for more on privacy.

Get connected

This chapter explains how to connect your computer to the Internet. You don't have a computer? Never mind, you'll find out how to choose one. You'll also learn how to choose a modem and an Internet service provider. Throw in a little software and you're on your way.

Covers

Chapter Two

Three simple steps

Now you know what the Internet is and where it came from, you're ready to get connected. It's time to make the giant leap from isolated individualism to interconnected bliss.

As with most giant leaps, connecting to the Internet is actually very easy. You don't have to throw yourself into the technological abyss, clutching this book to your chest. You just need to complete three simple steps and presto, you've joined the party:

1   **Sort out your computer.** If you don't have a computer, you'll need to get one. If you've just bought a computer, it probably came with everything you need to connect it to the Internet. If you've owned your computer for a couple of years, or you inherited it from another member of your family, you'll have to give it a once-over to see whether it's fit for the job. You must also decide whether you want a simple dial-up connection or a faster broadband one. Read pages 23–29 to find out more.

2   **Choose an Internet service provider (ISP).** Your service provider acts as a go-between, bridging the gap between your computer and the millions of others that are permanently connected together, forming the Internet. There are lots of ISPs, offering various levels of service, so you'll need to consider all the options and find a company that can make you happy. Pages 30–33 explain what to look for when you're choosing an ISP.

3   **Set up your software.** In most cases, setting up your software is as simple as inserting a CD from your service provider and clicking a couple of buttons. Sometimes you have to do a little more work. If you don't get a CD, or you want to transfer your Internet account to another computer, you may need to set up the software yourself. Follow the step-by-step guide on pages 34-36.

Choose a computer

You can connect to the Internet with almost any type of computer, but if you want an easy life, choose a Windows PC or an Apple Mac. You won't find much else in the shops, anyway.

Boring beige PC or trendy white Mac?

If you're trying to decide between a PC and a Mac, consider the following. Everyone hates PCs. Some people like Macs. Despite what the Mac people will tell you, Macs are no easier to use than PCs – but they look better in your living room. Nevertheless, PCs dominate the personal-computer market. If you have a problem, it's easy to find another PC user who can help. When you want to purchase software or hardware, you have many more choices.

The Internet looks much the same from either type of computer, although there is more software available for PCs.

Through the square window

This book concentrates on accessing the Internet from a Windows PC, because that's what most people have. If you're buying a new computer, get one with a fast processor, plenty of memory (RAM), a large hard disk and a display that gives you 16.7 million colors at a resolution of at least 1,024x768 pixels.

If you've just bought a computer, it'll have the latest version of the Windows operating system, Windows XP. If you have an older PC running an older version of Windows, such as Windows Me, Windows 98 or Windows 2000, think about upgrading. Windows XP includes new software that makes it easier to get connected.

The latest, greatest, newest version

To find out whether you have the latest version of Windows XP, click the Start button, then click Control Panel. Click "Performance and Maintenance", then click "See basic information about your computer". You will see which edition you have and which Service Packs are installed.

Microsoft has issued many updates for Windows XP since it was released in 2001. You'll need the very latest version, Windows XP Service Pack 2 (SP2), to use this book. If you have an older version, telephone Microsoft and order a free Service Pack 2 CD.

You can also download Service Pack 2 from Microsoft's Windows Update Web site (at http://windowsupdate.windows.com/) once you have connected your computer to the Internet. However, you'll only want to do this if you have opted for a fast broadband connection (see overleaf). It's better to get the update first, then connect your computer to the Internet.

Simple dial-up or speedy broadband?

The next thing to decide is how you are going to connect your computer to the Internet. There are two basic options: dial-up and broadband. If you want Internet access when you're on the move, you may also be interested in wireless connections.

Simple dial-up

A dial-up connection uses a modem to connect your computer to your telephone line, enabling you to "dial up" the Internet. This is the simplest option, because most new computers have modems fitted, so you don't need any extra hardware. Dial-up connections are inexpensive if you don't use the Internet very much.

The main drawback is that dial-up connections are slow, so you spend a lot of time staring blankly at the screen. Also, you cannot use your telephone line for voice conversations while you are connected to the Internet. See page 26 for more information.

Speedy broadband

A broadband connection is normally ten times faster than a dial-up connection, and it can be more than 100 times faster. Broadband makes the Internet more fun to use and enables you to download software, music and videos.

There are three types of broadband connection, although they may not all be available in your area. DSL services make the connection via your telephone line. Cable services use the fibre-optic cable that supplies your cable television signal. If you live in a remote area, you may need to connect your computer to a satellite dish and access the Internet via satellite broadband.

For a complete picture, you need to look at all the costs involved in the different types of connection, which vary from country to country. See page 31 for more information about paying for your Internet access.

You'll probably need to purchase additional hardware to set up a broadband connection, although you may be able to rent it from your service provider instead. Broadband connections are normally charged at a flat monthly rate, so they are expensive if you don't use the Internet very much, but good value if you use it a lot. See pages 27-28 for more on broadband connections.

The wonders of wirelessness

If you travel a lot and need Internet access wherever you go, you may want to connect wirelessly, using a cell phone. See page 29 for more on wireless connections.

Those mysterious numbers

This page will make your head hurt. It's only in the book because some people like to know exactly how fast their connection is. If you're happy with relative terms like "slow", "not so slow" and "really quite fast", you can skip ahead.

- The smallest unit of data is a bit. If you put eight bits together, you get the next unit, a byte. From there, data is accumulated into bigger, more familiar units. There are 1,024 bytes in a kilobyte (K or Kb), 1,024 kilobytes in a megabyte (Mb) and 1,024 megabytes in a gigabyte (Gb).

Hard-disk manufacturers aren't good at math and define a gigabyte as one billion bytes, even though the proper answer is 1,073,741,824 bytes. They believe (rightly) that you won't notice that you only have room for 19.1Gb of data on your 20Gb hard disk.

- File sizes are measured in kilobytes, or megabytes when you're dealing with large files such as video clips.

- Data-transfer speeds are measured in bits per second (bps). When you get up to 1,000bps, you have a transfer rate of one kilobit per second (kbps). When you reach 1,000kbps, you're transferring data at one megabit per second (Mbps). A rate of 1Mbps counts as "really quite fast". If your connection runs at 8Mbps, it is "really very fast", at least for 2005.

- Now things get tricky. A kilobyte is 1,024 bytes or 8,192 bits. A kilobit is only 1,000 bits. If your connection is running at 1kbps, it takes just over eight seconds to transfer 1K of data. In other words, a small "k" is different from a big "K".

- As a rough guide, you can work out how long it will take to transfer a file by dividing the connection speed by ten. A 56kbps connection can transfer 5–6K of data per second, so a 100K file takes about 20 seconds to download. Even less accurately, it takes about four minutes to download 1Mb of data. In practical terms, 1Mb equates to thousands of words, or a handful of digital photographs, or one minute of CD-quality music, or 10-20 seconds of video.

- To make things worse, people often abbreviate "kbps" to "K". A 56K connection is really a 56kbps connection.

- There are reasons why file sizes and data-transfer speeds are measured differently, but they're complicated to explain. Try to keep your "K"s and "k"s in order… and remember that your files will get there eventually, even if you don't.

Choose a modem

If you want to make a dial-up connection to the Internet, you'll need a modem – a box of electronics that converts computer data into audio signals that can be transmitted over a telephone line.

Once you've learned how to connect to the Internet, you can eavesdrop on your modem. Get connected, then pick up the handset of any telephone attached to the same line. You'll hear a hissing noise – that's your modem. Hang up before it gets upset and breaks the connection.

You can think of your modem as a very small office that houses a very small person who reads out the information from your computer. At the other end of the line, another very small person in another modem listens to the incoming data and keys it into the other computer. Occasionally the two people chat backwards and forwards to make sure everything is getting through. From a technological point of view, it's a strange way to communicate (see opposite for more advanced solutions), but it's cheap and it works.

In, out, shake it all about

Most new computers have an internal modem tucked away inside the system box (sometimes the modem is optional, so check before you buy). You also get a phone cable so you can connect the modem to a convenient telephone point.

For more information about the US Robotics V.92 Faxmodem USB (pictured), visit the company's Web site, at: http://www.usr.com/

If you need to buy a modem, get an external model that sits on your desk. It'll be easier to install than an internal one (you don't need a screwdriver, for starters) and you can move it from one computer to another. Pick one that connects to a USB port and you'll only need two cables – one to connect the computer to the modem and another to connect the modem to the phone point.

Make sure your new modem supports V.92, the latest standard for modem communications. A V.92 modem can download data at up to 56kbps (see previous page) and upload it at up to 48kbps. An older modem that uses the V.90 standard will also be okay, if that's what you have. A V.90 modem downloads at up to 56kbps and uploads at up to 31.2kbps.

"Download" means to copy information from the Internet to your computer. When you send information the other way, you "upload" it.

Choose broadband

The problem with modems is that they're slow. Computer data is converted into an analog signal, which creeps down the line and then has to be converted back into its original, digital form. What you really want is a high-speed digital connection.

A broadband service gives you a lot of "bandwidth" or data-carrying capacity. It's like having a wider road or a fatter pipe… you have a "broad" band.

Broadband services are the answer. If accessing the Internet with a modem is like filling a swimming pool with a garden hose, using broadband is like pumping water through one of the big, fat hoses that fire fighters use. Songs, videos and program files download in seconds instead of minutes, or minutes instead of hours. And with broadband, the Internet is always available, so you don't have to make a special effort to check your email, look at a weather forecast or track down a fact.

A broadband connection enables you to enjoy the movie trailers on Apple's Web site. Find them at: http://www.apple.com/trailers/

DSL: broadband via your phone line

Digital Subscriber Line is a relatively new technology that enables you to transmit digital data over a regular telephone line. Most services offer download speeds of 512kbps, 1Mbps or 2Mbps, making DSL 10-40 times faster than a modem connection. The upload speed is normally 256kbps, so you receive data faster than you can send it (the connection is asymmetric, so it's often called Asymmetric Digital Subscriber Line or ADSL). Most people download a lot more information than they upload, so that isn't normally a problem. What might be a problem, depending on where you live, is that you have to be within a few kilometers of a telephone exchange that supports DSL.

Beyond the speed, DSL has two advantages: the connection is "always on", so your computer can connect to the Internet whenever you power it up, and the data signal doesn't interfere with your phone conversations. You'll need a DSL modem or a combination modem/router, microfilters for all your telephone sockets and an ISP that supports DSL. Normally you pay a flat monthly fee, although some ISPs offer metered subscriptions that allow you to transfer a fixed amount of data.

Cable: broadband via the cable TV network

If you live in an area with cable TV, you have a nice fat fibre-optic cable running past your front door. Hook up a cable modem and you can use it to connect to the Internet.

Cable services offer download speeds of anything from 512kbps to 4Mbps or more (speeds of 30Mbps are theoretically possible). Upload speeds are lower, typically 256-512kbps. As with DSL, the connection is "always on" and doesn't interfere with your television and/or telephone services. One difference is that cable networks aren't as standardized as the telephone system and aren't open to competition. This means you'll have to get your Internet access (and possibly your modem) from the company that owns the cable network in your area.

Satellite: broadband out of the sky

If you live in a rural area, remote from telephone exchanges and cable networks, the only way to get high-speed Internet access is via satellite broadband.

There are two types of satellite setup: one-way and two-way. With a one-way setup, you receive data via a satellite dish, but you send it using a standard dial-up connection. This means you get fast downloads (typically 256-512kbps), but uploads run at normal modem speeds (30-48kbps). A one-way setup works well when you're browsing the Web, because you're mostly receiving data, but it's no good for sending large documents by email. With a two-way setup, you send and receive data via the satellite dish, so you get fast downloads and reasonably fast uploads.

The main disadvantage of satellite broadband is the cost. You have to pay for the dish (and probably for someone to come and install it) and the monthly costs are higher than for DSL or cable.

Snip the wires

If your job keeps you dashing hither and thither, collecting frequent-flyer miles and drinking bad coffee in gas stations, the main issue isn't the speed of your connection, but its portability. You need Internet-to-go, in the form of a wireless connection.

The Internet in your pocket

One option is to access the Internet using a cell phone. You need a special modem, either built in to the phone or installed in your laptop computer; a means of connecting your phone to the laptop (a cable, infrared or Bluetooth); and a certain amount of patience.

GSM stands for Global System for Mobile Communications. It's the most common system for digital cell phone networks. Find out more from the GSM Association's Web site, at: http://www.gsmworld.com/

If you are using a GSM network, your connection will be very, very slow. It'll be okay for collecting email, but you'll only want to use the Web in emergencies. For a more workable connection, look for a network offering General Packet Radio Service (GPRS), a newer system designed specifically for Internet-style data transfer. GPRS connections are not mind-bogglingly fast, but they're usable, and you can send and receive data while making voice calls. You're charged for the amount of information you transfer rather than the time you spend online. GPRS will eventually be replaced by Third Generation (3G) services that'll offer even faster connections… some day.

The Internet in your airport, café or hotel

Wi-Fi doesn't stand for anything. It's a marketing term used on products that conform to a particular wireless networking standard. Find out more about the joys of wireless networking from the Wireless LAN Association, at: http://www.wlana.org/

Another option is to fit a wireless networking card to your laptop and look for a Wi-Fi hotspot – a location where you can connect to a wireless network, which in turn connects you to the Internet. It's like using a public phone box, except you have to provide your own equipment. Most hotspots are located in areas where people sit around wasting time, such as airport lounges, coffee bars and conference centres. They're also starting to appear in libraries, museums, computer stores and the like – places where someone might get the urge to look something up on the Internet. You are normally charged according to the time spent connected.

Wi-Fi provides better connection speeds than a GPRS or 3G phone, but having to find a hotspot can be inconvenient (then again, maybe you were looking for an excuse to sneak off to your favorite café). If you're truly a road warrior, you probably want a cell phone with GPRS *and* a laptop with Wi-Fi.

Choose a service provider

Your Internet service provider is your new best friend. It reaches out a hand, enabling you to seize hold and become part of a giant chain of people (and computers) stretching all around the globe.

At your service

Internet service providers vary greatly. Some provide a bare-bones service aimed at expert users looking for a low-cost option. Others offer more support for beginners, or extra features for business people, or games servers for people who want to run around and shoot things. In general, though, an ISP does five things:

- **It provides connectivity.** Your service provider has powerful computers that are permanently connected to the Internet. When you want to use the Internet, you connect your computer to one of your ISP's computers, via the telephone system or cable TV network. Information passes from your computer to your modem, which sends it down the line to the ISP's modem, which passes it on to the ISP's computer, which sends it on to other computers – and vice versa. Your computer is (temporarily) part of the Internet.

- **It provides software, hardware and/or support.** If you have a new computer, you'll have all the software you need, but setting it up can be tricky. Some ISPs give you a setup CD that sorts everything out. Others help you over the telephone or have Web sites that answer your questions. If you opt for broadband, your ISP may provide a modem or router.

When your computer is connected to the Internet, it is "online". When it is not connected, it is "offline". Information can also be "online" (available on the Internet) or "offline" (not available).

- **It takes care of your mail.** You can only receive email while your computer is connected to the Internet. When it is offline, your ISP stores messages in an electronic mail box.

- **It provides a home for your Web pages.** If you want to create a Web site, you'll need to store it on a computer that's permanently connected to the Internet. Many ISPs give you a few megabytes of space that you can use for this purpose.

- **It provides additional services.** Most ISPs give you access to Usenet newsgroups (Chapter 10). Some offer extras such as game servers for multiplayer gaming, global roaming so you can access the Internet when you're overseas and registration of domain names (Internet addresses).

Everyone has their price

All this high-tech goodness is going to cost you something – maybe just a little, maybe a lot. In most countries there are lots of service providers, big and small, all competing furiously for your money. You'll need to sift through the deals to find one that suits.

There are two things you might have to pay for:

- The services provided by your ISP: connectivity, technical support, storage of mail and Web pages, and any extras it offers. This payment may also cover the hardware required for a broadband connection.

- The phone calls required to make a dial-up connection. In some countries local calls are free, or the call charges are collected by your ISP, so you only get one bill. In other places your phone calls can be most of the cost of a dial-up connection. If you opt for broadband, you don't have to worry about call charges.

There are three basic charging schemes:

- **Flat-rate, unmetered subscriptions.** This is the traditional charging scheme in countries where you pay for your local phone calls. You pay a flat monthly fee to your ISP and settle your phone bill separately (for a broadband connection, you just pay your ISP). There may also be a set-up fee when you open an account, especially if the ISP is providing hardware. The monthly fee gets you unlimited access to the full range of services, including technical support, and keeps the ISP on a firm financial footing.

- **Metered subscriptions.** When there's no charge for local calls, people spend more time on the Internet and ISPs have to ration their resources. Some offer subscriptions that let you use the Internet for a set number of hours each month, or (especially for broadband connections) transfer a fixed amount of data. If you go over your allotment, you pay an extra charge, on a per-minute or per-megabyte basis. You can usually change to a plan that offers more (or less) time or data if your Internet use changes.

Watch out for deals that seem too good to be true. An ISP that isn't making any money won't be able to invest in new equipment, won't offer a reliable service and may not be in business for long.

- **Pay as you go.** Some ISPs offer a "free" service. It costs nothing to open an account and there are no monthly charges; you just have to pay for your phone calls. The ISP funds its services through advertising or by taking a percentage of your call charges. If you need help and have to call the technical-support line, you're charged a premium rate to cover the cost of staffing the Help desk. Alternatively, you may be able to buy vouchers that entitle you to so many minutes or hours of Internet access. Once you've used up your time, you have to purchase another voucher.

You'll also come across more complicated offers that combine Internet access with other benefits, such as reduced rates for long-distance calls. **Always read the fine print very carefully.** Be wary of deals that require you to make a long-term commitment. You might not find the Internet useful, or you might use it more than you expect, or market conditions might change, making other packages more attractive.

The secret's in the sauce

To find out what's available in your area, flick through a couple of Internet magazines. You may find a directory listing all the local ISPs. If you don't, look at the ads.

There are lots of things to consider when you're comparing ISPs:

- **Price.** Try to work out how much you'll spend each month, including the cost of your phone calls, if applicable. As a rough guide, even a light user will spend 5–10 hours online. If you have school-age children or work from home, you might clock up anything from 25 to over 100 hours. When you're comparing broadband packages that restrict the amount of data you can download, remember that a four-minute music file weighs in at around 4Mb. Video clips require about 5Mb per minute and upgrading to Windows XP SP2 (see page 23) involves a 100-300Mb download.

- **Service.** How many email addresses do you get? It's nice to have a separate address for each member of the family. How big is your mail box? You don't want it to overflow if you go away for a few days. Can you access your mail via the Web (see page 144)? How much space do you get for your Web site? What extra features does the ISP offer?

- **Access numbers.** For a dial-up connection, make sure you can reach your ISP with a local phone call. If you'll be travelling with a laptop, look for an ISP that has access numbers in most areas or has roaming arrangements with other ISPs. Some ISPs offer special access numbers that are always charged at the same rate, no matter where you are.

- **Quality of the connection.** Check that your ISP supports the latest modem standard (V.92 at the time of writing). Make sure it has a low subscriber-to-modem ratio so there's always a modem to connect to. For broadband, check the contention ratio, which tells you how many people are sharing your bandwidth.

- **Technical support.** Find out how much you'll pay for calls to the helpline. Check the hours – a helpline that's open during working hours isn't much use if you plan to use the Internet in the evening and at weekends.

- **Flexibility.** If you're looking at dial-up services, find out whether you can switch to broadband in the future. Conversely, if you're getting broadband for your business, you might also want to be able to make dial-up connections when you're out on the road.

- **Terms and conditions.** All good ISPs have a set of terms and conditions, sometimes referred to as an "acceptable use policy". Make sure you can abide by the rules.

- **Reputation.** Any fool can set up an ISP. The difficult thing is providing a reliable, profitable service that keeps everyone happy, now and in the long term. Choose an ISP that has a well-established infrastructure and a good reputation. If possible, get a recommendation from a friend.

Changing ISPs is a nuisance – you may lose your email address, for example – but don't spend too long fretting over all the options. If things don't work out, you can try again. It's easier to make the right choice with some experience behind you.

Set up your software

It's time for the final phase of the Internet three-step: setting up the software. This is easier than it might sound.

Broadband connections aren't yet as standardized as dial-up ones, so you'll need to get specific instructions from your ISP, even if you're a computer whiz.

If you've opted for a DSL, cable or satellite connection, your ISP should help you install the hardware and set up your connection. You can skip ahead to Chapter 3.

For a dial-up connection, you'll probably get a CD from your ISP. Insert it into your PC and follow the on-screen instructions. The software on the disc configures your computer, telling it the phone number to dial and any special settings to use.

You may be asked to choose a user name and password. The user name forms part of your email address (see page 121), so choose it carefully. Your password should be easy to remember, but difficult for other people to guess (see page 98). Some service providers assign passwords automatically.

Do it yourself

You might need to set up a dial-up connection by hand. Your service provider may not give you a CD or you may want to transfer your connection to another computer. If you need to reinstall Windows, writing down and re-entering your details takes less time than hunting out a CD you haven't used for months.

Windows XP has a New Connection Wizard that helps you enter all the information your computer needs to make a dial-up connection. You'll need the following details:

It's a good idea to record all this information and keep it somewhere convenient – but not anywhere too obvious, because you should keep your password secret. If there's anything you don't know, call your service provider.

- Your service provider's phone number (the modem number, not the number you call to speak to someone).

- Your user name and password.

Later on, you'll also need:

- Your email address.

- The addresses of your service provider's mail servers (normally there are two, one for sending mail and another for receiving it).

- The address of your service provider's news server.

Dial-up connection wizardry

The New Connection Wizard provides step-by-step guidance for setting up a dial-up Internet connection.

1 Click the Start button and select All Programs> Accessories> Communications> New Connection Wizard

2 Click Next to continue (and after each step)

If you're setting up an office computer and will be dialing out through a switchboard, fill in the "If you dial a number to access an outside line..." section of the Location dialog box.

3 The Location Information dialog box may pop up. Select your country and enter your area code, if applicable, then click OK

4 When you get back to the New Connection Wizard, select "Connect to the Internet"

5 Select "Set up my connection manually"

6 Select "Connect using a dial-up modem"

7 Fill in the name of your Internet service provider

8 Enter your service provider's access number. Include the dialing code if it is different from your own dialing code

Turn to page 123 to find out how to set up Outlook Express so you can send and receive email. Page 157 explains how to set it up to access newsgroups.

9 Enter your user name and password. The password characters are hidden, so you have to enter it twice. Leave the bottom two options selected if everyone in the family is sharing your account. If other people will use their own accounts *from this computer*, deselect the first option

If you decide to have a shortcut icon on your desktop, you'll be able to connect to the Internet by double-clicking it. However, you won't normally need to do that, because Windows will prompt you to connect when you run an Internet program – see opposite.

10 If you want a shortcut icon on your desktop, select that option

11 Click Finish to create the connection and close the wizard

12 Click the Start button. You should have a Connect To option on the right-hand side of the Start menu

You can use the Connect To menu option to connect to the Internet – just select your service provider.

Dial up the Internet

When you run an Internet program, Windows checks whether you are connected to the Internet. If you aren't, it prompts you to dial your service provider.

1 To run Internet Explorer, the Web browser built in to Windows XP, click the Start button and select Internet from the left-hand side of the Start menu

2 The Dial-up Connection dialog box appears. Your user name and password should be filled in – if they aren't, enter them

3 Click the Connect button. You may hear your modem dial and then connect. Status messages appear at the bottom of the box

4 A yellow speech bubble lets you know that the connection has been established

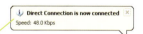

5 Internet Explorer displays a Web page like this, or a page from your service provider's Web site

6 You're ready to learn how to browse the Web (see Chapter 3)

7 When you have finished using the Internet, you need to disconnect. Go to the notification area at the right-hand end of the Windows taskbar. Look for an icon that shows two computers joined together

Don't get the Disconnect and Close buttons confused. When you click the Disconnect button, you end your Internet session. When you click Close, you simply close the dialog box, without disconnecting your computer from the Internet.

To check that you've disconnected correctly, pick up your telephone receiver. You should hear a normal dial tone. If you hear a roaring, hissing noise, you're still connected.

8 Double-click the icon to bring up the Status dialog box. Click the Disconnect button to close the connection

Ready, change settings, go

Your connection settings determine how and when your computer connects to the Internet. If you're using a dial-up connection, you can alter them so it only connects when you want it to and disconnects automatically when the connection is idle. That way you don't need to worry about running up your phone bill or missing important calls because you've accidentally left the computer connected.

1 Click the Start button and select Control Panel from the right-hand side. Select "Network and Internet Connections", then "Set up or change your Internet connection". The Internet Properties dialog box appears, with the Connections section at the front

2 If you have accounts with several service providers, all the possible connections are listed. Select the one you use most frequently and click Set Default

3 Select "Never dial…" to make connections manually using a shortcut icon or the Connect To section of the Start menu (see page 36). The "Always dial…" option enables your computer to make connections as required and is the best choice

4 To fine-tune the options for a particular ISP, select it and click Settings. This opens the dialog box shown overleaf

...cont'd

A proxy server stores copies of all the Web pages that have been viewed by people who have accounts with your service provider. If there's a copy of the page you want to see, your Web browser can download it from the proxy server more quickly than it could fetch it from the original Web site. In some countries proxy servers are also used to prevent people from accessing undesirable material.

5 If your service provider has a proxy server, select this checkbox and enter the address

6 If your user name or password changes, update your details here

7 If your service provider's phone number changes, click Properties and enter the new one

8 Click Advanced for further options

9 If all your service provider's modems are busy, your computer waits for a few seconds and then tries again. Tell it how many times to redial and how long to wait between attempts

10 Select "Disconnect if idle" to close the connection if you don't seem to be doing anything. You may want to reduce the idle time

11 Select "Disconnect when connection may no longer be needed" to end your session if you've closed all your Internet programs

12 Click OK three times to close all the dialog boxes

Click around the Web

The World Wide Web is the Internet's friendly face. It's colorful and attractive and provides straightforward, easy-clicking entertainment. This chapter covers the concept, the software and the addresses, then sends you off to browse.

Covers

Chapter Three

What is the Web?

The World Wide Web has been such a success that many people think it *is* the Internet. In reality, it's just one aspect of it – the prettiest and most popular one. Everyone likes the Web because it's attractive to look at, easy to use and packed with information.

But what is it, exactly?

The Web consists of over eight billion pages of text and graphics. Since they are designed to be viewed on a computer screen, they can also contain multimedia elements such as animations, sound files and video clips. It's like a gigantic, full-color magazine, with built-in speakers and a television screen in the center.

Web pages are held together by a system of electronic cross-references called hyperlinks. Instead of physically turning the pages, you use your mouse to click on a piece of text – or a graphic – that is electronically connected to another page. The beauty of this system is that it doesn't matter where the other page is located. It might be stored on the same computer as the first one, or on another computer on the other side of the globe. Also, one Web page can be linked to many others. The whole thing is held together by a tangled web of electronic connections that stretches all around the world – hence "World Wide Web".

If you know exactly where a Web page is stored, you can tell your computer the address and go straight to it. If you don't know the address, there are various ways to find it (you'll learn more about searching for information in Chapter 4). However, one of the great things about the Web is that you can find things you didn't know you were looking for, simply by following the hyperlinks. For example, you might start on a Web page about penguins, which points you towards an artist who makes paper penguins, who recommends the electronic incarnation of a British zoo, which diverts you to the BBC's Web site, and before you know it, you're reading about a new battery that makes electricity from leftover food.

A Web site is a collection of related Web pages. They all belong to the same person or company and they're all on the same topic.

Anyone can create a Web site, so there's a huge range of material to explore. Many newspapers publish an online edition. You can read the latest stories or click back in time to find out how a situation developed. Universities and museums use the Web to share information about their research and educate the public. Government organizations have sites that inform you about everything from political developments to parking charges and companies provide screeds of information about their products. You can check all the techy details before you hand over your cash.

Catch up on world news at the BBC News site, at http://news.bbc. co.uk/ or learn about Japanese culture at the British Museum, at http://www. thebritishmuseum.ac.uk/

There are also millions of Web pages created by private individuals who simply have a passion for their subject, be it penguins, pop stars or their personal, day-to-day life. Sometimes the Web feels like a giant scrapbook, packed with pictures and comments from anyone and everyone, be they famous or unknown, expert or amateur, completely ordinary or deeply strange. That's another great thing about it: you get a complete cross-section of views.

Choose a Web browser

You need a Web browser to view or "browse" the Web. It's a specialized piece of software designed to display Web pages and follow the links between them. Browsers also store the addresses of your favorite pages so you can find them again (see page 64).

The most popular Web browser is Microsoft's Internet Explorer. In second place is Mozilla's Firefox, a new program that's gaining popularity with more experienced Internet users. A small number of people use other browsers, notably Opera from Opera Software and Safari from Apple (for people with Apple Mac computers).

The two main browsers have many features in common. Web pages don't always look exactly the same in both programs, because some sites are designed to take advantage of the special features of one or other. However, it's unusual to see significant differences.

The BBC has created more than two million Web pages. Access them at: http://www.bbc.co.uk/

Internet Explorer

Firefox

This book concentrates on Internet Explorer, partly because of its popularity and partly because it's included with Windows, so most people have a copy. To learn more about the alternatives, visit the following Web sites:

Mozilla, at: http://www.mozilla.org/
Opera Software, at: http://www.opera.com/
Apple, at: http://www.apple.com/safari/

Internet Explorer at your service

If you use a CD from your service provider to set up your Internet connection (see page 34), it may customize Internet Explorer. Don't be alarmed if your version looks slightly different.

To run Internet Explorer, click the Start button and select it from the left-hand side of the Start menu.

Like most Windows programs, it has a title bar, menu bar and toolbars across the top of the window and a status bar at the bottom. The most important areas of the screen are:

Title bar – shows the name of the page

Menu bar

Standard buttons

Address bar – displays the address of the Web page

Links bar – buttons for popular Web sites

You can customize Internet Explorer by rearranging the toolbars or turning them off – see page 56.

Explorer bar – displays extra controls or information

Status bar

Main window, where Web pages are displayed

For news about Internet Explorer, plus how-to articles and advice, visit Microsoft's Web site, at: http:// www.microsoft.com/windows/ie/

Sometimes a pale yellow strip appears above the main window. It's called the Information bar and is covered on pages 78, 84 and 115.

Crack the address code

Once you're comfortable with Internet Explorer's interface, you're ready to go somewhere. Every Web page has a unique address, known as a Uniform Resource Locator (URL). You've probably seen Web addresses in newspapers and on television.

The address for Microsoft's Internet Explorer Web page is:

  Address **http://www.microsoft.com/windows/ie/default.mspx**

HTTP is short for HyperText Transfer Protocol, a set of rules for transferring Web pages. If you see an address beginning with https, you're looking at a secure Web page – see page 96.

The http: indicates that you're dealing with a Web page

This is the name of the Web server – the computer where the page is stored

This section tells your browser which folder the page is stored in

This is the name of the document that describes the page

Internet Explorer assumes you are looking for a Web page, so you don't have to type the http:// at the beginning. If you're looking for the main page of a company's site, you can also leave out everything after the first single slash. To find the main page of Microsoft's Web site, you would enter: www.microsoft.com

Understanding Web addresses

You don't have to understand how Web addresses are constructed, you just have to type them correctly. However, they can provide clues about where a page is located and who it belongs to.

Web addresses never contain spaces, but they can include hyphens and some other punctuation. Sometimes they are case sensitive, so if you see a capital "T" in an address, don't type a lower-case "t".

The name of the Web server usually has three or four sections:

www.microsoft.com
www.bbc.co.uk

The first section (www) is used to distinguish between different computers belonging to the same organization. It's known as a host name. The middle section (microsoft or bbc) is usually the owner's name. The last section (.com) or last two sections (.co.uk) tell you what type of organization owns the address, and sometimes where it is located. Collectively, the last two or three sections (microsoft.com or bbc.co.uk) are known as a domain name.

The rules for domain names reflect the haphazard evolution of the Internet. The most common single-section endings are:

There are three "global" top-level domains that are reserved for US organizations. They are .edu (education), .gov (government) and .mil (military).

.com	commercial entity (but also used by individuals)
.org	organization (usually non-profit)
.net	Internet-related business (such as an ISP)
.int	international body (such as the United Nations)

These endings are known as global top-level domains, because the owner can be based anywhere in the world. Seven new ones have recently been added: .aero (air transport), .biz (businesses), .coop (cooperatives), .info (information), .museum (museums), .name (individuals) and .pro (professionals).

The .us country code isn't used very often. Most US businesses and organizations use the .com and .org top-level domains instead.

Two-section endings consist of an organization code and a country code: .us (United States), .uk (United Kingdom), .fr (France), .de (Germany), .ca (Canada), .au (Australia), .nz (New Zealand), .sg (Singapore) and so on. The organization codes differ from country to country. In the UK, the most common endings are:

.co.uk	equivalent to .com
.org.uk	equivalent to .org
.net.uk	equivalent to .net
.ac.uk	academic institution (but not a school, which would have a .sch.uk address)
.gov.uk	government

For a complete list of country codes, visit the Web site of the Internet Assigned Numbers Authority (IANA), at: http://www.iana.org/cctld/cctld.htm

Other countries have similar organization codes, although it's quite common to use .com instead of .co and .edu in place of .ac.

If you don't know an organization's Web address, you can quite often guess it, simply by following the rules. For example, suppose you're looking for the Singapore Web site of electronics giant Sony. Two possibilities spring to mind:

http://www.sony.co.sg/
http://www.sony.com.sg/

If you try them both, you'll find the second address is correct.

Enter an address

If you know the address of the Web page you wish to visit, enter it into Internet Explorer. There are three ways to do this:

If you type ineasysteps and press Ctrl+Enter, www. and .com are added for you.

1   Type the address into the Address bar, then click the Go button or press the Enter key. Internet Explorer finds and displays the Web page

You can also click the arrow at the right-hand end of the Address bar for a list of addresses you've entered recently. This list only shows addresses you've typed yourself.

2   Once you've visited a few sites, Internet Explorer tries to anticipate your typing. If you see the right address in the drop-down list, click on it. You don't have to press Enter

If you don't want Internet Explorer to complete your addresses, turn off this feature under Tools>Internet Options> Content>AutoComplete. To clear the list of addresses, go to Tools>Internet Options>General and click Clear History.

3   The third option is to select Open from the File menu or press Ctrl+O. Both actions bring up the Open dialog box. Type an address or select one from the list. Click OK

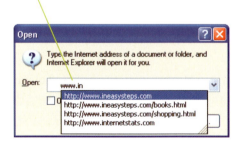

Oh no, it didn't work!

The Internet is constantly evolving: Web sites come and go and computers are moved or upgraded. It's also subject to bugs and bad connections, so sometimes Internet Explorer gives you an error message instead of displaying the page you want to see.

Don't be surprised if you see something quite different. Some Web sites have their own error messages with more specific information.

Sometimes you will find yourself looking at a Web page that's quite different from the one you expected. Some Webmasters take advantage of common typing errors to attract you to their sites. Others take over the addresses of sites that no longer exist.

The vast majority of errors arise because:

- You've typed the address incorrectly. Try again, checking the characters carefully before you click Go or press Enter.

- The computer where the page is stored is temporarily out of action. Try again in a few hours.

- The page you want has moved. If this is the case, Internet Explorer displays the address of the main page of the Web site. Click it and try to find the page from there.

Click the links

If you could only get to Web pages by typing in addresses, browsing the Web would be time-consuming and tedious. Fortunately you can use hyperlinks to get about more quickly.

Almost every Web page is linked to anything from one to a dozen or more other pages. Links are usually indicated by colored, underlined text, and you move to the linked page by clicking this text. For example:

To find out more about Google, turn to page 61 or visit its Web site, at: http://www.google.com/

Here's a page from Google's Web directory. If you click the blue, underlined text that says "Computers"…

Normally the new page replaces the old one. If you want to display both pages at once, hold down Shift when you click the link, or right-click the link and select Open in New Window from the pop-up menu.

2 …you are taken to this page, which lists the Computers subcategories. Choose a topic and click again to go to another page

Links can also take you to another section of the same page, to save you scrolling up and down.

Linked text isn't always blue or underlined. However, you can tell when the mouse pointer is over a link, because it changes into a pointing hand ☝. The linked text changes color after you've clicked it so you can see where you've been.

Graphics can be used as links – see page 75.

Quick ways to get about

It's easy to get disorientated when you're browsing the Web. There are lots of directions to head in and it's hard to remember where you've been. Internet Explorer helps you retrace your steps.

1 To return to the page you just left, click the Back button or press Alt+Left Arrow

You can use the History bar to return to any page you've visited in the last two or three weeks – see page 67.

2 To go back several pages, click the arrow to the right of the Back button. Select the page you want to revisit from the drop-down list

3 Once you've gone back a few pages, you may want to go forward again. Click the Forward button or press Alt+Right Arrow. To go forward several pages, click the arrow to the right of the Forward button

4 If you get lost, you can start again by clicking the Home button or pressing Alt+Home. This takes you to your home page – the page Internet Explorer looks for each time you run it (see page 70)

The logo in the top right corner is animated when a page is downloading and becomes static when the transfer is complete. You can click on links as soon as you see the text – you don't have to wait for the rest of the page to arrive.

5 If a Web page is taking too long to appear, click the Stop button, select View>Stop or press Esc to abort the download

6 If you change your mind and want to see the rest of a half-downloaded page, click the Refresh button, select View>Refresh or press F5 to reload the page. You should also click Refresh if you think Internet Explorer isn't displaying a page correctly

Print a Web page

If you're gathering information for a report or project, you might want to print out relevant Web pages.

You can also click the Print button on the toolbar, but you'll bypass the Print dialog box.

1 To print the current page, pull down the File menu and select Print. Alternatively, press Ctrl+P

2 Decide whether to print the whole document or specified pages (see opposite)

If you're only interested in a couple of paragraphs of text, highlight them with the mouse before you go to File>Print. In Step 2, choose "Selection".

3 If the page has frames (see page 91), click the Options tab

4 Decide whether to print all the frames, or just the selected one (the one you clicked in most recently)

5 Click the Print button to print the page

Print Preview

Because Web pages are designed to be viewed on a monitor, they don't always print the way you expect them to. If you use Internet Explorer's Print Preview function, you get more control over the output. You can see whether the document will be printed on several sheets of paper and select the pages you want to print.

1 To preview your printout, select File>Print Preview

To decode the header and footer codes in the Setup box, click the Help button ? in the top right corner, then click on the "Header" or "Footer" settings.

2 To change the margins, header, footer and/or page orientation, click the Setup button 🗔

3 Use this set of controls to move from page to page

4 Use this set of controls to zoom in or out

Look out for links or buttons that take you to "printer friendly" versions of longer articles. The printer-friendly version may condense several pages into a single document and/or use a simpler layout.

5 Once you're happy, click the Print button

6 Use the "Print range" option (Step 2, previous page) to print specific pages

Make yourself at home

Internet Explorer's toolbars are very flexible. You can arrange the Menu bar, Standard buttons, Address bar and Links bar to suit yourself, or turn off some of these toolbars to create more space.

You can also turn toolbars on or off from View>Toolbars.

1 To turn off a toolbar, right-click on an empty section of the Standard buttons. A pop-up menu appears. Deselect the toolbar you no longer want to display

2 If there is a check mark beside Lock the Toolbars, the toolbars are locked. Deselect this option to unlock them

To make your mark on the Standard buttons, right click on an empty section of this toolbar and select Customize... from the pop-up menu. You can add and remove buttons and change their order and size.

3 To move a toolbar, use your mouse to grab the gray handle at the left-hand end. Drag it up, down or across

4 You can have several toolbars on the same line

Turn to page 69 to find out more about the Links bar.

5 To expand a toolbar so it occupies the full width of the window, double-click on its handle. Double-click again to put it away

6 If you find you're moving the toolbars by accident, right-click on an empty section and reselect Lock the Toolbars

Lost and found

You've been browsing the Web for hours and you still haven't found what you were looking for. Time for another chapter, then. This one shows you how to avoid the dead-ends and diversions and go straight to a relevant Web site. It also explains how to record the locations of useful sites so you can find them again quickly.

Covers

Chapter Four

Finding information

Imagine visiting an enormous bookstore, with shelving spread out over ten floors and millions of books on every conceivable subject, all at bargain prices. Sounds fabulous… except the books are arranged in no particular order. The novels are mixed up with the nonfiction and the books aren't sorted by author or subject. How frustrated are you? Very!

Sometimes the World Wide Web feels like that. You know the information you need is out there somewhere, but finding it involves sifting through billions of Web pages spread out over millions of computers. You can't just follow the links from page to page – your children's children might be growing old by the time you reach your destination. You need a way to find information more quickly.

The Web has two answers: directories and search engines. Directories are like Yellow Pages for the Internet. They list Web sites by topic and subtopic, enabling you to focus in on the area of interest. For example, if you're looking for an explanation of Albert Einstein's Theory of Relativity, you select Science, and then Physics, Relativity and so on. Web directories work well when you're researching a broad area.

Search engines are more efficient when you're looking for specific information. They enable you to search through a vast database that indexes all the text on every Web page. You type in a few words – "Albert", "Einstein" and "relativity", perhaps – and the site produces a list of all the Web pages where they appear. In most cases you get a brief extract that helps you work out which pages are relevant. If you choose your words with care, you can jump straight to a Web site that answers your question.

Big Web sites often have mini search engines that only index their own pages. You'll also come across specialized search engines that accept queries in plain English or look for specific types of material, such as news stories, pictures or music files.

Web directories

Web directories are intuitive and easy to use. You select the category that best describes the information you're looking for, then select the most relevant subcategory, and so on.

The Yahoo! Web directory started out as a list of useful Web sites put together by David Filo and Jerry Yang, students at Stanford University. Their personal "sort out the Internet" project has evolved into a behemoth that's one of the best-known and most-visited sites on the Web. These days it's far more than a directory and you'll have to push your way past numerous other services to find the lists of Web sites. Nevertheless, it's a good place to start if you want to browse the Web by category.

Yahoo! also has local directories for many regions and countries. Try some of these:

- *Yahoo! UK & Ireland*
  http://uk.yahoo.com/
- *Yahoo! Australia & NZ*
  http://au.yahoo.com/
- *Yahoo! Canada*
  http://ca.yahoo.com/
- *Yahoo! Singapore*
  http://sg.yahoo.com/

1 Skip past the main site at: http://www.yahoo.com/ and go straight to the directory at http://dir.yahoo.com/

2 Suppose you want to find a site about Albert Einstein's theory of relativity. Click the "Science" link

3 You get a new set of categories. Select "Physics"

4 The Physics subcategories are displayed. Select "Relativity"

5 The Relativity categories include "Albert Einstein"

The purple bar at the top of the page shows your location in the Yahoo! directory.
The directory is cross-referenced, so you could also have reached this page by clicking "Science", "Physics", "Physicists" and "Einstein, Albert".

6 The Albert Einstein category lists around 20 Web sites. Click the links to start exploring.

7 Look out for the blue "Pick" logo, which highlights sites chosen as Yahoo!'s "Pick of the Day".

The American Museum of Natural History has an online exhibition about Albert Einstein, at: http://www.amnh.org/exhibitions/einstein/

Search engines

Search engines are more efficient but not as intuitive. You spend less time clicking and more time thinking, a trade-off that might not seem appealing on a lazy Sunday afternoon. However, once you've mastered a search engine, you can get results very quickly.

Google was also born at Stanford (a university that attracts neat geeks and makes them tidy up the Internet). Founders Larry Page and Sergey Brin set out to create a system for retrieving the best and most relevant Web pages on any given topic.

Like most search engines, Google aims to index every word on every Web page. Uniquely, it ranks Web pages according to the number of links that point to them – so if a lot of people like a Web page and link to it, the page gets a good ranking. It's very efficient and has a simple, uncluttered design.

The name Google is a play on googol, the mathematical name for a very large number consisting of a one followed by 100 zeros.

Like Yahoo!, Google has localized versions that let you concentrate on sites in your own country. It often redirects you to a local version when you visit the main site.

The words you enter are known as "keywords" or "search terms". Internet Explorer remembers the words you have entered previously – see the HOT TIP on page 91.

If you're a gambler, click the I'm Feeling Lucky button in Step 3. You'll bypass the list and go straight to the top-ranked Web page.

1 To use Google, visit the main page of its Web site, at: http://www.google.com/

2 Enter a word (or words) in the text box

3 Click the Google Search button

4 You get a list of pages that include your words. Try following a few of the links

5 You get ten results on each page. Use the links at the bottom (or click the yellow "o"s) to move through the pages

6 To modify the search, edit your words in the box at the bottom (or top) of the page, then click Google Search again

Always add the quotes when you're looking for a specific sequence of common words.

7 To search for a phrase, enclose it in double quotes (" ")

8 Google only lists pages that contain your words in that exact sequence

Searching the Internet involves getting into the mindset of a computer – a machine that can process vast quantities of data but can't think laterally. Remember that the search engine knows nothing about your subject and you'll find it easier to get results.

Successful searching

Searching the Internet can be frustrating, but with practice you'll be able to locate information quickly and efficiently.

Bear the following in mind:

Internet Explorer has a built-in search feature – click the Search button to activate it. It's easy to use but not as efficient as Google.

- Decide whether you're searching or browsing. If you're looking for general information about a broad topic, such as relativity, use a directory to find sites that concentrate on that subject. If you're looking for a specific person or event, use a search engine.

- Read the instructions! Most search engines have special features that help you refine your search. However, they're all different and what works with one won't necessarily work with another. Once you've found a search engine you like, stick with it – the others may find a slightly different selection of sites, but you won't miss much.

- Think words, not concepts. Search engines look for Web pages that contain your keywords, so don't try to describe the concept. You'll get better results by thinking of terms that are likely to appear in the text of a relevant page.

- Refine your search with phrases and extra terms. Most engines allow you to specify that two or more words should appear together, or that the Web pages must contain some words and not others.

- Be specific. If you cast your net too widely, you'll pull in lots of rubbish.

- Use alternatives. Try "film" as well as "movie" and don't forget that "football" refers to different games in different parts of the world.

- Check your spelling, especially when you're entering names. Some search engines are case sensitive and will distinguish between "Reed" and "reed". If you're uncertain, use lower case for everything except proper names.

- Use specialized services, if appropriate. For example, Google has options that enable you to search for images, news stories or messages posted in Usenet newsgroups (see Chapter 10).

Favorite places

Once you've gone to all the trouble of finding a useful Web site, you'll want to remember where it is. Rather than writing down the address, add the site to Internet Explorer's Favorites menu.

1 To create a Favorite for the current page, select Add to Favorites from the Favorites menu

Find out all you ever wanted to know about movies from the vast and immensely popular Internet Movie Database, at: http://www.imdb.com/

2 Check the name – you may want to change it to something shorter

You can also right-click on the page and select Add to Favorites from the pop-up menu. Right-click on a link to create a Favorite for the Web page at the other end.

3 Click OK to create the Favorite

4 You can return to this page whenever you want, simply by selecting it from the Favorites menu

Keep things tidy

Before long your Favorites menu will be as much of a mess as the Internet. To tidy it up, organize the entries into folders. This creates submenus and makes it easier to find the site you want.

1 Go to Favorites> Organize Favorites

You'll already have a Links folder – see page 69.

2 Click the Create Folder button

3 Type in a name and press Enter

You can also drag Favorites to the correct folders.

4 Select a Favorite that needs to be moved into the new folder. Internet Explorer displays its details on the left

5 Click Move to Folder

6 Select the folder. Click OK to go back to the Organize Favorites dialog box

7 Click Close to finish organizing your Favorites

To save a new Favorite straight into a folder, click the Create in>> button (see Step 2 on page 64). Select the folder, then click OK.

8 Your Favorites menu now has submenus. To access a folder, hold the mouse pointer over its menu entry until the submenu appears

You can also reorganize your Favorites by dragging them around with the mouse. Open the menu and point to an entry with the mouse. Press and hold the left mouse button, pause for a second or two, and then drag the Favorite or folder to a new location. You can move it to a specific position by looking out for the black divider that appears when the mouse pointer is between two items.

9 To sort your Favorites and folders into alphabetical order, open the Favorites menu and right-click on it. Select Sort by Name from the pop-up menu

10 Repeat for each of your submenus

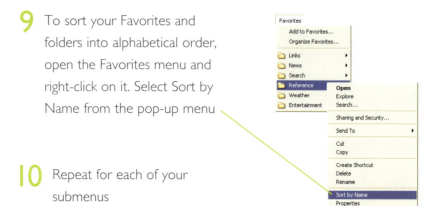

All your Web sites in a bar

The Favorites bar gives you another way to view and organize your Favorites. It's more convenient than the menu, but it intrudes on the main window.

1 Click the Favorites button to open the Favorites bar

Click the Organize button to bring up the dialog box shown in Step 1 on the previous page. You can also drag your Favorites around the bar to reorganize them.

2 Click a folder to see a list of Favorites

3 Click a Favorite to open a Web page in the main window

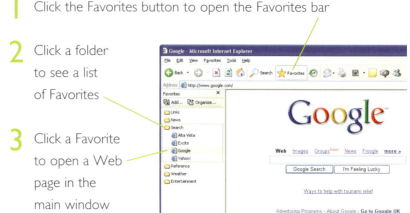

Ancient history

If there's any chance you might want to return to a page, it's a good idea to make a Favorite for it. However, all isn't lost if you forget. You can use the History bar to return to pages you've visited in the last couple of weeks.

To tell Internet Explorer how long to keep the records for, go to Tools>Internet Options and click the General tab. In the "History" section, specify the number of days.

1 Click the History button to open the History bar

2 Click the correct day, then click the site where the page resides

3 Click the title of the page to load it into the main window

4 If you can't find the page you want to see, click the View button to sort the History bar another way

5 Select By Site if you know where a page was, but can't remember when you last visited it

6 Or, use By Most Visited to bring your favorite sites to the top

7 Or, use By Order Visited Today to review today's browsing

8 Still no luck? Click the Search button instead. Enter a keyword and click Search Now to hunt through your history

Internet Shortcuts

An Internet Shortcut is a Favorite that lives on your Windows desktop, rather than in the Favorites menu. Double-click on it to run Internet Explorer, connect your computer to the Internet and go to the specified page.

Internet Shortcuts are useful for sites you go to frequently. For example, you could use a Shortcut to CNN's Web site to start Internet Explorer first thing in the morning. Later in the day you might want to use a search engine or visit an entertainment site.

If you can see your desktop alongside Internet Explorer's window, you can make Shortcuts using the "page" icon *at the left-hand end of the Address bar. Drag it on to the desktop to make a Shortcut for the page. This trick is handy when you want to make a temporary note of the address of a Web page.*

To create an Internet Shortcut, right-click on the background of the Web page and select Create Shortcut from the pop-up menu. Alternatively, go to File>Send>Shortcut To Desktop

A dialog box appears. Click OK to create the Shortcut

To rename the Shortcut, click on it once, wait a couple of seconds and then click again on the text. Type in a short, descriptive name.

The Shortcut is placed on your desktop. Double-click it to start Internet Explorer and load the specified page (if Internet Explorer is already running, double-clicking the Shortcut just takes you to the page)

Links bar

The Links bar provides another way to access your favorite sites. Initially it contains buttons for sites selected by Microsoft or your service provider. You can replace these with your own top choices.

| To display the Links bar, double-click on its handle (see page 56)

2 If you don't find the default links useful, right-click on them and select Delete from the pop-up menu

You can also create a new button by using your mouse to drag the page icon 🅔 from the Address bar to the Links bar.

3 There are lots of ways to create new buttons. To add the current page, select Add to Favorites from the Favorites menu. Click the Create in>> button and select the Links folder

Why do some sites have fancy icons? This is up to the Web designer – if they create a special icon, Internet Explorer uses it.

4 Alternatively, open the Favorites bar and drag a Favorite on to the Links bar. Place it between the existing buttons – a black divider appears when the mouse is in the right place

Home page

Internet Explorer looks for the home page each time you run it. You're also taken to this page when you click the Home button or press Alt+Home.

The default home page is usually one of your Internet service provider's Web pages, although you may be taken to one of Microsoft's Web pages instead. You don't have to stick with the default setting – you can change the home page to any page you visit often or find useful, such as a news site or search engine.

1 To change the home page, browse to the site you'd like to use. Select Tools>Internet Options and click the General tab

2 Click Use Current to change your home page

3 Or, click Use Default to revert to the home page that was specified when you installed Internet Explorer

4 Or, click Use Blank if you often want to run Internet Explorer without connecting to the Internet. It will load a blank page from your hard disk instead of running the connection software

Lights, camera, cue music, action

Like the pages in a book or magazine, Web pages can include pictures – no surprises there. Unlike printed pages, however, they can also include sounds, music, animations, videos and other interactive goodies. This chapter explains how to enjoy the fun stuff that brings the Web to life.

Covers

Chapter Five

Multimedia mayhem

Before the Web, the Internet consisted almost entirely of words and numbers. If you wanted anything as exotic as an image or a sound bite, you had to know how to find it and what to do with it once you'd copied it on to your hard disk. Multimedia wasn't even a word, let alone something any ordinary person could enjoy.

The illustrated history

The first Web browsers couldn't display pictures. Then, in 1993, along came a browser called Mosaic. It was able to combine text and images, enabling people to create (moderately) attractive Web pages. Mosaic gave birth to a program called Netscape Navigator, a distant relative of today's Firefox. Navigator's success prompted Microsoft to create Internet Explorer, and the rest is history.

Images changed the face of the Web. They made it colorful and interesting, gave it personality and boosted its appeal. When the Internet was a big heap of words, no-one wanted to cover it in newspapers, let alone on television. Now it pops up everywhere.

For everything you ever wanted to know about the US space program, along with lots of still images, sounds and videos, visit NASA's Web site at: http://www.nasa.gov/

The Web in 1997…

…and in its current glory

Sum of its parts

A Web page looks like a single document, but it's really a patchwork of different files. When you enter a Web address, your browser downloads a document that contains the text, plus instructions for displaying the page. The instructions are written in HyperText Mark-up Language (HTML), a special language used to format text and add hyperlinks. They also include details of any images that need to be inserted. Once your browser has read the instructions, it downloads the images and assembles the page.

Each image is stored in a separate file, so a Web page with three pictures is put together from four files: one that contains the text, plus three more for the images. This "sum of the parts" approach explains why the text usually appears first. Until it reads the instructions, your browser doesn't know anything about pictures.

The full works

Once there were pictures, people started to think it would be cool if you could attach sound samples to Web pages. Why settle for a picture of Charlie Chaplin when you could be listening to him say… no, maybe that isn't the best example. But how about a video clip from one of his movies? That would be better than a still.

Today's Web browsers don't just display static pages. They can also handle sounds, music, videos and animations. You can watch highlights from a big sporting event, look at stills of the decisive moments, listen to an interview with a key player and read the opinions of expert commentators. It's better than being there.

Newer, better, faster, more

As with images, each sound bite or video clip is stored in a separate file. The problem is that people keep inventing new ways to store this type of material. There are dozens of different formats for sounds and videos, and the list just keeps growing. A Web browser can't be expected to recognize all the different types of multimedia file, let alone know how to handle them.

A helper application displays extra material in its own window. Plug-ins and ActiveX controls are more tightly integrated with the browser and the multimedia file is blended into the Web page.

Programmers have developed a nifty way to sidestep this problem. When a browser encounters a file it doesn't understand, it hands it off to another program. These extra programs are known as helper applications, plug-ins or ActiveX controls.

You can think of the extra programs as the electronic equivalent of extra blades for your food processor. Each time you want to do something new, you install a small program that enables Internet Explorer to slice, dice, shred and otherwise process the data. Most of the add-on programs are free and straightforward to install.

File formats

This is another technical diversion that you can skip if you aren't in the mood. However, it's easier to make sense of multimedia if you know a little bit about file formats.

A file format is a set of rules for storing a particular type of information. There are different formats for text documents, numerical data, pictures, sounds, video clips and so on. What's more, there are lots of different formats for each type of data.

On a PC, the format of a file is indicated by a three-letter extension at the end of the filename. For example, story.txt is a basic text file, whereas This is my life.doc is a Microsoft Word document. The extension is separated from the main section of the filename by a dot. Other types of computer have different rules, so you may encounter longer file extensions on the Internet. On a PC, the proper extension for a Web-page document is .htm, but on some other systems it is .html

Windows has an annoying habit of hiding these extensions, but you can take control and force it to display them.

1 Click the Start button and select My Computer from the menu

2 Go to the Tools menu and select Folder Options. Click the View tab

3 Scroll down the Advanced Options list until you find "Hide extensions for known file types". Click this option to deselect it

4 Now you can see what you're dealing with!

File extensions are often used to describe files. For example, a friend might offer to email you a .jpg of their kids. What they're really offering you is an image file in the JPEG format.

The right image

There are three standard file formats for images on the Web: .gif, .jpg (.jpeg on systems that have longer extensions) and .png.

You might think there isn't much to viewing images. You open a Web page, you look at the pictures, end of story. To be honest, that's all you *need* to do… but there are a few extra tricks that are worth knowing.

Click the pictures

Images aren't just used to make Web pages pretty. They can also help you get from one place to the next. Web designers can turn images into links so a click takes you to another Web page, or sometimes to another image.

There are three common types of linked images:

Many Web sites have their logo at the top of each page. Clicking the logo usually takes you back to the main page.

- **Buttons.** Many Web sites use icons and toolbars to help you navigate. For example, Yahoo! (see page 59) has buttons that take you to special sections of the site.

- **Image maps.** Some images contain more than one link. For example, the Aardman Animations site opens with this wall of graffiti. It looks like a single image, but clicking on the scribbles takes you to different parts of the site. You might come across group photographs where you can click on each person to go to their Web page.

Experience the power of plasticine with Aardman Animations, at: http://www.aardman.com/

- **Thumbnails.** Large images take a long time to download, so Web designers often show you small preview versions first. For example, NASA's Earth Observatory Web site has a gallery displaying small versions of the latest images. Clicking on one of the small images takes you to a larger version with additional information.

Find hundreds of satellite images on the Earth Observatory Web site, at:
http://earthobservatory.nasa.gov/

If you see an icon with a red cross ☒ where an image should be, Internet Explorer either can't find or can't display the image file.

Not sure whether an image is linked to anything? Move the mouse pointer over it. It turns into a hand 🖑 if the image is clickable.

Image toolbar

If you hold the mouse pointer over an image, without clicking, a toolbar may appear. It makes it easy to do things with the image.

1 Save the image

2 Print the image

3 Attach the image to an email message so you can send it to a friend (see Chapter 8)

4 Open the My Pictures folder

Sometimes another button appears in the bottom right-hand corner of the image. It only shows up when you're viewing an image on its own, rather than as part of a Web page. It appears because Internet Explorer has resized the image to fit it into the window.

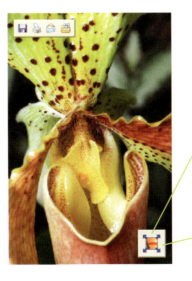

1 Click the button to expand the image to its normal size. Use the scroll bars to move around

2 Click again to make the image fit into the window

Animated antics

Some animations are similar to image files. Internet Explorer automatically inserts them into the page. Others are saved in a specialized animation format and require add-on software.

Very flash

The Flash format is used for intro screens, animated menus and special effects. It has become very popular because the files are small and download quickly. The software for creating Flash animations comes from Macromedia.

You need to install Flash Player to view Flash animations. The simplest option is to get it from Macromedia's Web site.

1 Visit Macromedia's Web site at: http://www.macromedia.com/ Go to the Downloads section and click the link for Flash Player

2 Click the Install Now button

The Information bar displays a warning whenever a Web site tries to send you a program file you didn't specifically request. See Chapter 7 for more on downloading program files.

3 The yellow Information bar appears at the top of the window. Click it and select Install ActiveX control

Whenever you see a warning message like the one in Step 4, check the name of the program and the name of the company that published it. If you aren't sure what the program does or you don't recognize the company, click Don't Install to abort the installation.

4 A dialog box warns you that a program is being downloaded. Click Install to proceed

5 When the player is ready to use, a brief animation informs you that installation is complete

If you visit a Web site with Flash animations before you install the player, Internet Explorer may display a message in the Information bar, telling you the Flash Player is required. Follow Steps 3 and 4 (previous page) to install it. Alternatively, the Web site may have a button or link you can click to start the installation procedure.

You can view animations as soon as the installation is complete. You don't have to restart your computer or close Internet Explorer. The Flash Player just does its stuff, automatically, whenever it is required. You don't see it working, you only see the results.

Shockingly good

People often confuse Flash and Shockwave. They both come from Macromedia and they do similar things. However, they aren't interchangeable – you need both of them to enjoy all the multimedia on the Web.

Flash has a big brother called Shockwave. Like big brothers the world over, it's more sophisticated than its sibling and can be used to combine text, graphics, animation, digital video and sound into games, interactive movies and multimedia documentaries.

You need the Shockwave Player to view Shockwave files. You install it in exactly the same way as the Flash Player (except you click the link for Shockwave Player, obviously).

Wonderville 3D uses both Flash and Shockwave to create a 3D environment that encourages kids to learn about science and technology. Find it at: http://www.wonderville.ca/

Make some noise

The Internet is alive with the sound of music… and people talking, birds singing, swords clanging, phasers firing and many other sci-fi sound effects. Audio is used to inform and educate, to entertain and to provide atmosphere.

There are many different file formats used for sounds, but they can be divided into two basic groups:

- **High-quality sound formats** such as .wav (Windows audio), .mp3, .mid (or .midi), .aif (or .aiff), .au and .snd. These formats are used for short sound bites, synthesized music and CD-quality recordings. You have to download the file before you can play the sound.

- **Streaming sound formats** such as .ra and .ram (from RealNetworks) and .wma (used by Windows Media Player). These formats are designed to deliver audio in real time. The data is compressed so one minute of sound takes one minute to download. The audio "stream" is played as it arrives and there's no waiting around. Streaming formats are used for recorded sound, live broadcasts and Internet radio.

Playing sound clips

With a little help from Windows Media Player, Internet Explorer can play sound clips in the high-quality, non-streaming formats.

To play a sound clip, click the link that leads to it

The Daily .WAV provides daily sound bites from movies and TV shows. Find it at: http://www.dailywav.com/

2 Sometimes the page is designed so the clip plays within Internet Explorer. A set of playback controls may appear within the page

To change the style of the Windows Media Player window, click Skin Chooser and pick a design.

3 It's more common for the clip to be transferred to Windows Media Player

If the sound breaks up, play the clip again. It may play more smoothly.

4 Use the tape-deck style controls to adjust the volume or replay the clip

Setting up Windows Media Player

If you have problems playing sound files, you may need to change some of the settings in Windows Media Player.

Installing other sound or video players may change some of the settings in Windows Media Player, making it harder to play sound clips in Internet Explorer.

1 If you see a dialog box like this when you try to play a sound clip, Windows Media Player is not set up to play this type of file. Check the file type, then click Cancel

To run Windows Media Player, click the Start button, then click All Programs. Select Windows Media Player from the list of programs.

2 Switch to Windows Media Player. Right click on the pale blue bar at the top of the window and select Tools>Options.

3 Click the File Types tab. Make sure there is a check mark beside the type of file you want to play

4 Try to play the sound clip again

System sounds include the fanfare that plays when you turn on your computer and the beep that announces that you've done something wrong. To change these sounds, open Control Panel and select "Sounds, Speech and Audio Devices". On the next page, select "Change the sound scheme".

Saving sound clips

Sometimes you'll want to save a sound clip to your hard disk. You might want to keep a copy so you can play it again in the future or use it to replace one of your system sounds.

1 To save a sound clip, right-click on the link that leads to it. Select Save Target As from the pop-up menu

2 Choose a folder for the file and make sure it has a sensible name – one you'll recognize later on

3 Click Save

4 Once the download is complete, click the Open button to play the file

5 Or, click Open Folder to open the folder, or Close to go on saving files

There is nothing inherently evil about the MP3 format. It's only controversial because it has been used to distribute pirated music.

What's so special about MP3?

You might have noticed a big fuss about the MP3 format over the last few years. The music business has been waving its arms in the air and wailing, mostly because of the copyright issues.

When music is saved in the MP3 format, all the sounds you don't normally hear are removed. If a loud note and a soft note are played at the same time, and the pitch is similar, the loud note masks the soft one, so there's no need to record both sounds. Eliminating the redundant sounds reduces the size of the file by a factor of around 12. This means that a four-minute song can be squeezed into a 4Mb .mp3 file, without sacrificing the sound quality. Purists with expensive hi-fis can tell the difference, but the music is good enough to play around the house or in your car.

If you have a 56kbps modem, a 4Mb file takes 12–15 minutes to download. On a high-speed broadband connection, the download takes about a minute.

For more information about digital music and reviews of software and services, visit MP3.com, at: http://www.mp3.com/

MP3 is great if you want to record a song and put it on your Web site for everyone to enjoy. It doesn't have quite the same appeal for record companies. It's easy (but illegal) to convert music from a CD into a collection of .mp3 files and share them with other Internet users, saving them the bother and expense of purchasing their own discs. However, it's hard for musicians to earn a living if everyone is getting music for nothing – hence the controversy.

Some record companies now sell digital music, either in MP3 format or in similar, proprietary formats. You can purchase single tracks or entire albums. You get the convenience of immediate downloads and the warm glow of legality.

You can play .mp3 files with Windows Media Player. It's best to save large files to your hard disk, then play them (see opposite). Some people prefer to use a specialist MP3 program such as Winamp (from Nullsoft at http://www.nullsoft.com/) or iTunes (from Apple at http://www.apple.com/itunes/).

Portable MP3 players such as Apple's iPod are similar to personal stereos, but use memory or a hard disk instead of tapes or CDs. You download music from the Internet (or create .mp3 files from your own CDs) and transfer it from your computer to the player.

Streaming sound

Playing streaming sound is similar to playing clips (see page 80). There are three main differences:

- You don't have to wait for the sound file to download.

- Depending on the format, you may need extra software.

- You can't normally save streaming sound.

Some Web sites transmit streaming sound in Windows Media format. You play the stream using Windows Media Player. Others use the RealAudio format, which requires RealPlayer. Get it from the RealNetworks Web site, Real.com, at: http://www.real.com/

There are two versions of RealPlayer: a basic version, which is free, and a "Plus" version, which you have to pay for. You may have to look carefully to find the link for the free version.

1 Visit Real.com and follow the links for the free player

2 When you reach the download page, the Information bar pops up. Click it and select Installation Blocked>Install ActiveX Control

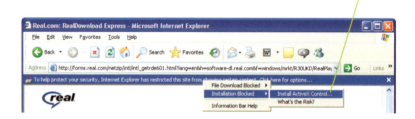

3 A security warning appears. Check the details and click Install if you want to continue

4 The setup program is downloaded and the installation routine starts automatically. Follow the on-screen instructions to install the RealPlayer software

Tuning in to Internet broadcasts

Streaming sound can be used for prerecorded material, such as interviews, or for live broadcasts. For example, many radio stations stream their broadcasts to listeners all over the world.

Listen to BBC Radio – both live and prerecorded – by following the links from its Web site. Find it at: http://www.bbc.co.uk/radio/

1 To play prerecorded material or tune in to a live broadcast, click the button or link that leads to it

2 There is a short pause while your computer locates the stream and then the broadcast begins to play

3 Use the controls to pause the playback and adjust the volume

There are lots of different ways to present streaming sound. Some sites have simple links that activate Windows Media Player or RealPlayer; others have customized player windows like the BBC Radio Player console shown above. When in doubt, click the link and see what happens!

Watch a video

Just as TV is more captivating than radio, videos are more fun than sound clips. However, video files are also much larger than audio files and take much longer to download. To make the most of all the videos on the Web, you need a broadband connection.

The most popular application for videos is movie trailers. You can get sneak previews of new films, long before they reach your local cinema, simply by browsing the Web. You can also watch sports highlights and documentaries.

Apple has a special section of its Web site devoted to movie trailers. Find it at:
http://www.apple.com/trailers/

Playing videos is very similar to playing sounds:

- You click a link to download the video and activate a player.

- There are many formats for video files. Some have to be downloaded before you play them; others can be streamed.

- You need more than one player to view everything.

Some video files can be played in Windows Media Player, some require RealPlayer and others need a player you've yet to encounter: QuickTime Player (see opposite).

File format	Best player
.asf, .wmv (Windows Media)	Windows Media Player
.rm, .ram (RealMedia)	RealPlayer
.mov, .qt (QuickTime movies)	QuickTime Player
.avi, .mpg (or .mpeg)	Any of the three players

If you install all three players, the right one will be activated when you click a link that leads to a video file.

...cont'd

Like RealPlayer (see page 84), the QuickTime Player comes in two flavors. There's a basic, free version and a "Pro" version that you have to pay for. When this book was written, the easiest way to get the free version was by downloading iTunes, Apple's digital music program. By the time you read this, QuickTime player may be available separately. Visit the QuickTime section of Apple's Web site for the latest version.

Installing QuickTime Player

You can download QuickTime Player from Apple's Web site, at:
http://www.apple.com/quicktime/

1 Visit Apple's Web site and follow the links for the QuickTime Player

2 Select the correct version

3 Scroll down and enter your details

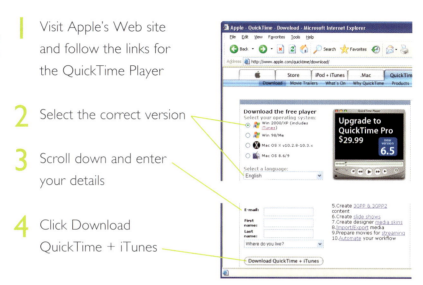

4 Click Download QuickTime + iTunes

You clicked a button to start the download, so the Information bar does not appear. It only pops up when a Web site tries to start a download automatically.

5 When the warning appears, check the details. If everything looks okay, click Save to proceed. Choose a folder and click OK

6 Once the download is complete, click the Open Folder button. Double-click the icon to start the setup routine

7 Follow the on-screen instructions to complete the installation

To find out which add-ons are installed in your browser, go to Tools> Manage Add-ons…

You've now installed three different add-ons in three different ways. Flash Player was downloaded and installed automatically (see page 78). RealPlayer was downloaded automatically, but you had to help with the installation (see page 84). Finally, QuickTime Player had to be downloaded first, then installed by hand

...cont'd

Playing video clips

The exact procedure for playing a video clip depends on the format, but clicking the link that leads to it is always a good start.

The NASA site is unusual. Most Web sites only provide videos in one or two formats. Find these videos at: http://spaceflight.nasa.gov/

| NASA's Spaceflight Web site offers some movies in all three formats

QuickTime videos can also be integrated into Web pages that include text, images and so on.

2 If you click the QuickTime link, the video clip is played in the center of the browser window

To save a video clip, follow the instructions for saving sound clips on page 82. Saving video files to your hard disk before you play them often gives better results than playing them directly off the Web. As with sounds, some types of video file can't be saved.

3 If you click the Windows Media link, the video clip is played in Windows Media Player

4 If you click the Real Video link, the clip is played in RealPlayer

Streaming video

Since streaming sound is used for Internet radio, you might expect streaming video to be used for Internet television – and you'd be right. The catch is that video involves a lot more data than sound, so it's much harder to crush the files to the point where one minute of video takes one minute to download with a 56kbps modem. It's really only feasible when there isn't much happening in the video – for example, when it consists of someone reading the news. More dynamic broadcasts have to be compressed to the point where all you get is a sequence of disjointed frames.

A high-speed broadband connection can carry at least ten times as much data as a modem connection. Broadcasts designed for this type of connection don't have to be compressed as much and they're a lot easier to watch.

BBC News broadcasts video bulletins from its Web site, at: http://news.bbc.co.uk/

Playing streaming video is just like playing streaming sound. Follow the instructions on page 85, or just click the link that leads to the broadcast and see what happens. If you can't find anything to watch, try the following sites:

Real Guide, at: http://guide.real.com/
WindowsMedia.com, at: http://www.windowsmedia.com/

A panoramic view

A panoramic image provides a 360-degree view of a scene or location. When you view the image, you feel as if you're standing next to the photographer. You can spin round and look in any direction, or zoom in or out, and sometimes there are clickable hotspots that take you on to other images. Panoramas are used to show you the interiors of houses, hotels and museums; to put you into areas of outstanding natural beauty; and to take you to places you're unlikely to visit personally, such as the surface of Mars.

Panoramic images are created by taking a series of overlapping photographs, then stitching them together into cylinder or sphere. Since the final image isn't flat, you need special software to view it.

There are two common formats for panoramic images:

• **QuickTime Virtual Reality** (QuickTime VR or QTVR). The files have a .mov extension and are viewed with QuickTime Player – see page 86.

• **iPIX**. These files have a .ipx extension and are viewed with the iPIX plug-in, which is available from the iPIX Web site at: http://www.ipix.com/ The plug-in installs itself, just like Flash Player – follow the instructions on page 78.

Once you've installed the viewers, panoramas are downloaded and displayed automatically.

Take a virtual tour of the Louvre on the museum's Web site. The tour uses the QTVR format, enabling you to spin round inside the rooms and approach the artworks. Find it at: http://www.louvre.fr/

1 To explore the image, hold down the mouse button and pan left, right, up or down

2 To zoom in or out, press Shift or Ctrl (QTVR) or use the plus (+) or minus (−) keys (iPIX)

Interactive Web pages

Web designers can also spice up their pages by adding interactive elements such as pop-up menus, forms, calculators and simple games. Some of these items are built in to the document that describes the page; others are downloaded separately and dropped into place by your Web browser.

Fill in the form

Internet Explorer can remember all the things you've typed into forms. When you start typing a keyword into a search engine, for example, it may display a list of similar words you've typed before. If one of the entries on the list is correct, click it. To turn this feature on or off, or clear the list of entries, go to Tools>Internet Options. Click the Content tab, then click the AutoComplete button.

Forms enable you to enter keywords into search engines and fill out questionnaires. However, they aren't all dry and serious. They are also used for interactive gadgets such as automatic letter writers.

Forms are just like dialog boxes, except the text boxes, drop-down lists, radio buttons and check boxes are part of the Web page. Once you have filled in the blanks, you click a button to send the data back to the computer that hosts the Web site. You'll get a response – another Web page – a few seconds later.

Here's a fare-checking form from United Airlines:

Check flight times and fares on the United Airlines Web site, at http://www.united.com/

Text boxes

Radio buttons

Drop-down list

When you fill in your requirements and click the Search button, you're given a list of suitable flights.

You've been framed

Frames divide the main window into two or more "panes" that can be scrolled or updated separately. They enable Web designers to display several documents at once. Clicking a link in one of the frames can change its contents, or change the contents of the other frames, or take you to an entirely different Web page.

Normally you'll see gray dividing bars between the panes, but it's possible for the designer to make the divisions invisible.

Many people find frames annoying, because they are disorientating and make it difficult to print Web pages. They aren't as popular as they used to be and you won't come across them very often.

Follow the script

It's possible for a malicious programmer to use scripts to access private information or cause problems on your computer – see page 117 for more on this and similar hazards.

A script is a set of instructions that is included in a Web page. You don't see the script on the screen, but it tells Internet Explorer what to do when you click a button or enter some text. Scripts are used to display dialog boxes, carry out simple calculations and add special effects such as scrolling messages. They can also change the formatting of a Web page at a specified time, or in response to your mouse movements, mouse clicks and keystrokes. Items can appear or disappear, move around, change color and so on.

You're most likely to notice scripts when something goes wrong. If Internet Explorer comes across instructions it doesn't understand, it displays an error symbol at the left-hand end of the Status bar. Sometimes you can ignore the problem – you may still be able to get the information you need, even though the page isn't being displayed properly. If you can't, all you can do is email the site's designer with details of the error.

Enjoy a cup of Java

Java was developed by Sun Microsystems. To find out more or see some applets in action, visit the company's Web site, at: http://java.sun.com/

Java is a programming language that enables Web designers to create small programs or "applets" that can be added to Web pages. Like image files, applets are stored separately from the main Web-page document and slotted into place by your browser.

The thing that makes Java special – and the reason there's been some hype about it – is that a single Java program can run on many different types of computer. It's a two-part system: as well as the applets, you have the Java Virtual Machine, which is built in to your browser. It acts as an interpreter, converting the standard code into something your computer understands.

Java hasn't been as successful as people expected, so it's possible to use the Web for months without encountering an applet. If you do come across one, it'll run automatically.

It's a rich man's world

People used to think the Internet was all about sex… but they were wrong, it's all about shopping. You can buy everything from books, CDs, videos and popcorn to bookshelves, hi-fis, video recorders and microwave ovens… and then apply for a credit card, overdraft or mortgage. Chapter 6 shows you how to empty your wallet without losing your shirt.

Covers

Chapter Six

Spend and save

In real life, spending and saving go on opposite sides of your personal profit-and-loss statement. Money you spend is money you don't save, and vice versa.

On the Internet, shopping and banking have a lot in common. In both cases, you protect your assets by keeping your personal details private. No matter how generous you are, there are some things you don't want to share – and your credit card and bank account numbers are high on the list. Whether you're spending money in online stores or moving it from one account to another, Web browsers encrypt your instructions so they pass across the Internet safely, away from prying eyes.

Shop until you drop

Online shopping has a lot to offer, both for shopaholics and for people who have to be dragged into town on a leash:

- **It's convenient.** You can order almost anything, at any time of the day, and have it delivered to your door.

- **It's efficient.** Rival stores are only a mouse-click apart. And once you're inside, you don't have to traipse about, trying to work out whether the socks are near the shoes (which would be logical) or in some separate universe (which seems more likely). If you can't find them, click the Search button.

British stalwart Marks & Spencer sells socks over the Internet from its Web site, at: http://www.marksandspencer.com/ and US bookseller Barnes & Noble sells books about socks (and many other things), at: http://www.barnesandnoble.com/

- **You can browse in peace.** Even when an online store is busy, you feel as if you're the only customer. You don't have to push through the crowds and shop assistants don't pop out from behind the racks to ask if they can "help" you.

- **There's lots of information.** Some stores don't just tell you about their products, they also allow other customers to record their opinions. And if you want a detailed technical specification, you can click across to the manufacturer's site.

- **The range is amazing.** The Internet has everything from big-name department stores to specialist dealers selling items that are far too obscure for your local shopping mall.

- **It's global.** You can buy all sorts of things from all sorts of countries. And when your friends move to New Zealand and have a baby, you can order a cuddly toy from a store in their part of the world.

- **You'll save money.** Online stores don't have the overheads of their real-world rivals, so they can offer better deals.

The only drawback is that you can't handle the merchandise. It's difficult to tell whether your butt will look big in a dress you've ordered online, although most stores offer exchanges or refunds.

Personal banking

If you have any money left after your online spree, Internet banking is the answer. You can:

- check your balance.

- transfer money between accounts.

- pay most of your bills.

It's much more efficient than writing checks and putting them in the post. You can see exactly what's happening in your accounts, even at two in the morning, and it's easy to stay on top of things.

Safe and secure

Shopping and banking inevitably involve transmitting your credit card number and bank account details over the Internet. Before you do that, though, you need to make sure they won't go astray.

Do not enter your credit card number into insecure forms or include it in email messages. The same rules apply to any other confidential information.

Shops and banks that do business online use secure servers to collect sensitive information. When you're accessing a Web page on a secure server, all the data you send is encrypted to protect it from eavesdroppers. Sophisticated mathematical procedures turn confidential information into gibberish and then unravel it again at the other end. Anyone who tries to intercept the transmission ends up none the wiser.

Secure connections are slower than regular ones, so shops normally use an ordinary server for their product pages, then switch you over to a secure one when you're ready to make a purchase – usually as you approach the checkout. Banks use secure connections for anything that is specific to your account, including balance checks, transfers and bill payments. Product brochures and marketing fluff live on an ordinary server.

There are several ways to identify a secure server:

Internet Explorer informs you that you're opening a secure connection. The warning message should appear before you are asked for your credit card number

...cont'd

2 Check the Address bar. Secure Web addresses begin with https:// rather than the usual http://

If a Web site uses frames (see page 91), it's hard to tell whether it is secure. Right-click within the frame that holds the order form and select Properties to check the status of the connection.

4 Double-click the padlock to see the site's security certificate. Check the address – it should match the site you're viewing

3 A padlock icon appears at the right-hand end of the Status bar

5 Internet Explorer displays another warning when you leave the secure server

Get into the habit of checking for the warning messages and padlock before you make a transaction. Some people turn off the warnings (by selecting the "In the future, do not show this warning" check boxes), but it's better to leave them on. Online shopping and banking warrant both a belt (the warning messages) and braces (the padlock icon).

Passwords

Passwords are the bane of Internet users' lives. If you aren't thinking up a password for a site you've just discovered, you're trying to recall the one you chose last week.

Many online shops keep a record of your payment and shipping details so you don't have to re-enter them every time you buy something. When you're ready to make a purchase, you enter your user name and password and the site "remembers" who you are and where you live. Banks also use password systems to confirm your identity. They tend to be stricter about the form of your password, but the principle is the same.

If you start using message boards (see Chapter 10), you'll need a user name and password for each one. Some regular Web sites also require you to log on, so they can keep track of your visits. Before you know it, you've got dozens of passwords to remember.

Choosing passwords

Never reveal the password that you use to connect to the Net to anyone you meet online, even if they claim that they work for your service provider and need your details to prevent a problem with your account. Anyone who asks for this information is up to no good.

You can use the same user name on lots of different Web sites. Some sites use your email address to identify you, which makes life even easier (unless you have lots of email addresses and can't remember which one you used). However, you should use a different password each time. That way if someone does manage to work out your password for a particular site, they don't get access to anything else.

There are two common ways for someone to break your password: they can guess it, or they can use a program that works through a dictionary, trying every word. Try to choose passwords that are immune to both types of attack.

- Don't use your name or user name, or the names or nicknames of your partner, children or pets.

- Don't use your date of birth, ID number, telephone number, licence plate or any other easily obtainable information.

- Don't use place names or any word found in a dictionary.

- Use a mixture of letters, numbers and punctuation (if permitted). Use both uppercase and lowercase letters and make each password at least six characters long.

• One good option is to choose a consonant, then add one or two vowels, then choose another consonant, and so on until you have a nonsense word that's meaningless but pronounceable (which makes it easier to remember). For example, you might use "zigoonad" or "rumiatop".

• Another trick is to think of two short words, then separate them with a number or punctuation character, producing passwords such as "cat8cups" or "run$free".

Remembering passwords

If you log on to the Internet from home and lead a blameless life, choosing good passwords is less important than finding some way to remember the ones you've already picked.

Internet Explorer can remember many passwords for you. It doesn't do this by default; instead, it asks if you want this feature turned on the first time you type a password into a Web site. If you click Yes, it offers to remember each password you enter.

You may want to use this feature for sites where your password simply gives you access. It's less of a good thing on shopping sites, because it may enable family members to access your account and make purchases with your credit card.

1 To turn off this feature, go to Tools>Internet Options. Click the Content tab, then click the AutoComplete button

2 Deselect the "User names and passwords" option

3 You can also clear the password list

Sensible shopping

Online shopping is convenient, easy and fun… but it isn't quite like going to a real-world shopping mall. There are different things to watch out for and the whole process may seem strange at first. To make sure your online shopping expeditions are safe and successful, stick to a few simple rules:

- **Start somewhere familiar.** For your first few purchases, stick to companies you know or sites recommended by people you trust. Once you've learned how to recognize a reputable shop, you can be more adventurous.

- **Look around the Web site before you buy.** Can you find the company's street address and phone number? How much will delivery cost? What happens if your items aren't in stock? Will the company take the goods back if there's a problem? Good shopping sites provide plenty of details about their services. Look for a Customer Service, Help or FAQ (Frequently Asked Questions) section and read through it carefully.

US store DVD Empire sells DVDs, games and CDs from its Web site. Find it at: http://www.dvdempire.com/

Read the small print before you make a purchase

- **Make contact.** If you aren't sure about a company, ask for a catalog or call up with a question. See how the company treats a potential customer: do you get a quick and helpful response or an unwelcoming silence?

- **Use your credit card.** Always pay with a credit card – you have more protection when you do. Check with the issuer of

your card to find out exactly what your rights and
responsibilities are.

- **Double-check your order before you submit it.** Have
  you selected the right size, the right color and/or the right
  number of items? For that matter, have you selected the
  right items? It's easier to make mistakes when you don't have
  the goods in your hands.

*Fat Face sells
casual clothes for
men and women,
at: http://www.
fatface.com/*

Check all the
details of your
order carefully

- **Keep a record of your transactions.** Print out details of your
  order (see page 52) and file any confirmation emails you
  receive. Usually there'll be an order number that you can
  quote if you have any queries.

- **Check your credit card statements.** Go through your bill
  each month and make sure you can account for all the
  purchases. If you see a retailer or amount that you don't
  recognize, call your credit card company. Be doubly vigilant
  if you pay your bills automatically with a direct transfer from
  your bank account. It's easier for a rogue purchase to slip
  past if you aren't writing a check each month.

Internet shopping can save you time and money and enable you to
buy things you wouldn't normally get in the shops. Don't be put
off by all these warnings – if you shop sensibly, it can be safer than
walking down the street with a bulging wallet in your back pocket.

Buying from overseas

The ease with which you can make purchases from overseas is one of the special joys of Internet shopping. You can buy specialist items that aren't available locally; take advantage of lower prices in other countries; or order presents for friends and relations who live elsewhere. However, there are some special considerations when you shop overseas:

- **Will they deliver, and how much will it cost?** Before you get all excited about tracking down the final item for your priceless collection of whatever, find out whether the store delivers to your country. If it does, check the cost – you may need to ask for a quote. Shipping costs can be surprisingly reasonable or staggeringly exorbitant, depending on the delivery method, and it pays to shop around.

- **Will it work?** Be particularly careful when purchasing electrical equipment, telephone equipment, anything involving radio signals (including radio-controlled toys), videos and DVDs. Standards for these items vary from country to country.

- **Is it guaranteed?** What happens if something goes wrong? Do you have to ship the item(s) back to the country of origin? Dealing with overseas merchants is almost always more hassle than dealing with local companies and the costs can mount up. Avoid buying items that might break down. It's better to purchase them in your own country, even if you have to pay a little extra.

- **Will you have to pay duty and/or tax?** Your fabulous bargain may not seem as attractive when it's accompanied by a big bill from your local tax and customs people. On the other hand, you may be able to avoid sales tax in the country of origin. Do the sums before you submit your order.

Brochures and forms

As well as being a great place to shop, the Internet comes in handy when you need to research your purchases.

Most big companies have Web sites, and if they manufacture products or provide services, you can be pretty sure they'll be promoting them online. Many companies provide everything from photographs to detailed technical specifications to lists of the available colors – far more information than you'd get from most shop assistants. There's a better chance of it being right, too.

Companies that have printed brochures sometimes provide online versions in PDF format. A .pdf file is an electronic facsimile of a paper document. You can view it, using a program called Adobe Reader, and you can print it, but you can't edit it.

Get Adobe Reader from Adobe's site at: http://www.adobe.com/

PDF is short for Portable Document Format. It was designed to enable people to share documents even if they were using different software on different types of computer. Unlike Web pages, which are designed to be viewed on the screen, PDF files are optimized for printing. The designer has more control over the layout, so they can make the pages look nice or cram in lots of details.

1 Follow the links to the download page and select the correct version of Adobe Reader. Download it on to your hard disk (see Chapter 7)

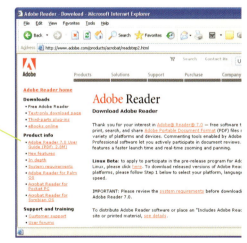

2 Open the folder containing the downloaded program and double-click on it. You may have to wait while extra files are downloaded

3 Follow the on-screen instructions to install Adobe Reader

The PDF format is also used for application forms. If you want to open a new bank account, for example, you may be able to download the application form from the bank's Web site, print it out, fill it in and send it off.

You can run Adobe Reader as a stand-alone program or use it from inside Internet Explorer.

Suppose you want to look at one of the product brochures on Adobe's Web site.

1 Click the link that leads to the .pdf file to open it in Internet Explorer

2 Adobe Reader's toolbars appear inside Internet Explorer's main window. Use the tools to view, save and/or print the document

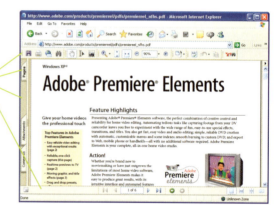

3 When you're finished, use Internet Explorer's tools to navigate back to the original Web page or on to somewhere else

4 Alternatively, right-click on the link to the .pdf file and select Save Target As to save it on to your hard disk

5 Open the folder that contains the .pdf file and double-click it

6 The file is opened in a stand-alone Adobe Reader window

Fancy filework

The Net is awash with free software, try-before-you-buy-ware and add-ons and upgrades for commercial programs. This chapter explains how to grab all the files you want without downloading the things you certainly don't want: viruses, Trojan horses and worms.

Covers

Chapter Seven

Get your free software here!

If there's one thing Internet users have in common, it's computers. Like it or loathe it, almost everyone who uses the Net is beholden to a computer of some sort. And if there's one thing computer users have in common, it's their rapacious appetite for software. Seems as if you're always short of a program to do this or a utility to do that. Unsurprisingly, the Internet has evolved into a giant buffet that enables you to pile your plate with new software.

You'll find six different types of software on the Internet:

- **Commercial programs.** Instead of buying shrink-wrapped boxes from a computer store, you can purchase software online. You pay with your credit card (see Chapter 6), then download the program on to your hard disk.

- **Demos and trial versions.** Many software companies appreciate that using a program tells you a lot more than reading about it. Rather than trying to describe their whiz-bang new application, they let you download a trial version. Most demos lack one or two key features. For example, you may not be able to save or print your documents.

- **Add-ons and upgrades.** Software companies also use the Internet to distribute freebies such as utilities, document templates and "patches" that fix minor problems.

- **Drivers.** A driver is a small program that enables your computer to communicate with an add-on device such as a printer or a camera. Drivers get updated regularly.

The shareware system relies on people paying for the programs they find useful. The registration fees help pay for further development, leading to new versions with extra features. If you use a shareware program regularly, do the decent thing and send the programmer some money.

- **Shareware.** Shareware programs are distributed on a "try before you buy" basis. You're allowed to use a shareware program for a while to find out whether you like it (unlike a trial version, it should give you access to all the important features). If you find it useful, you pay a registration fee. You'll usually get an enhanced version with extra features as a reward for your support.

- **Freeware.** The Internet is full of small programs you can simply download and use, free of charge. Some are too small to be worth marketing commercially. Others are produced by hobby programmers who enjoy sharing their creations.

Find your programs

Downloading programs is easy (see overleaf). Finding software to download can be a little more challenging, especially if you have a particular task in mind, rather than a specific program.

If you're looking for commercial programs, demos, add-ons and upgrades or driver software, start by visiting the software or hardware company's Web site. Usually you can guess the address. For example:

Adobe is at: http://www.adobe.com/
Epson is at: http://www.epson.com/
Symantec is at: http://www.symantec.com/

Spot the pattern? If guessing doesn't work, use a search engine (see page 61). Once you've found the site, look for a Products, Support or Downloads section.

Sometimes you need a program to do a particular job. For example, you might be looking for an icon editor. Start by visiting one of the sites that catalog downloadable software. Two of the best are:

Download.com, at: http://www.download.com/
Tucows, at: http://www.tucows.com/

Download.com has details of thousands of programs

These sites let you search by program name or keyword. You can find all the icon editors, then use the descriptions, reviews and user ratings to make a decision. Either download the program directly or click through to the developer's Web site for more details.

Haul down the files

Internet Explorer enables you to fetch and run a program in a single operation, but you'll almost always want to save it on to your hard disk instead. You can experiment with your new software once you've disconnected from the Internet.

Find Herman Compute's Icon Editor program at: http://www. hermancompute.com/

1 To download a program file, click the link that leads to it

There's always a chance that a downloaded program might contain a virus. Don't click the Open button unless you are absolutely, positively, utterly sure the program doesn't contain anything nasty. When you click the Save button, you can use your antivirus software to check the file before you open it (see page 111).

2 Internet Explorer asks whether you want to open (run) the file or save it on to your hard disk. Click Save

3 The standard Save As dialog box appears. Select a folder and click the Save button

4 The file is downloaded on to your hard disk – this often takes several minutes. You can continue browsing or switch to another program and carry on working

...cont'd

5 Once the download is complete, you have three options. Click Run to run the program straight away

Your antivirus software should automatically scan any file you download from the Internet. If it doesn't, scan the file manually before you open it – and get a better antivirus program.

6 Or, click Open Folder to find the downloaded file on your hard disk. Double-click on the program's icon to run it

7 Or, click Close to close the dialog box and go on with something else. Don't forget to deal with your new program later on!

Compressed files

Software companies often use compression programs to "archive" the program files linked to their pages. Creating an archive packs everything – setup utility, documentation, help files and the program itself – into a single, neat package. The archive is smaller than the original group of files, so it downloads more quickly.

See page 74 for more about file extensions.

The most popular compression programs produce archives with a .zip extension. Follow the instructions on the previous two pages to save them on to your hard disk.

Once you have downloaded a .zip file, you'll need to decompress or "unzip" it.

1 Open the folder containing the file. Double-click it

You may also come across other types of archive. Self-extracting archives have an .exe extension and unzip themselves automatically when you double-click the original file. Archives with names ending in .hqx, .sit, .sea, .gz, .Z, .tar or .gtar contain Apple Macintosh or Unix files. It's unlikely you'll be able to use the files in these archives, so it's best to avoid them.

2 Windows displays the contents of the .zip file. To unzip it, click "Extract all files"

3 The Extraction Wizard helps you unpack the files into a new folder

Keep your computer healthy

There are several types of malicious programs, including viruses, worms and Trojan horses. A virus attaches itself to other programs. A worm can replicate independently and doesn't need to attach itself to a program. Trojans don't replicate – they just cause damage if you make the mistake of running them.

A computer virus is a small piece of program code that attaches itself to other programs. When you run the infected program, the virus copies itself to another program or causes your computer to do something untoward. Some are just irritating, but others may damage or destroy your files.

Programs versus data

A program file contains instructions for your computer. When you run the program file, for example by double-clicking it, your computer follows the instructions.

Data files contain information. Many data files are associated with particular programs. For example, Windows normally associates .jpg (photograph) files with Windows Fax and Picture Viewer. When you double-click a data file, Windows runs the associated program and displays the data – in this case, the photograph.

Viruses attach themselves to program files. When your computer runs the program file, it carries out all the normal instructions, plus some extra ones added by the virus. This is how viruses make copies of themselves or cause strange things to happen – they weave their instructions into other programs.

How do you tell the difference between a program file and a data file? It isn't always easy. Try looking at the file extension. If the filename ends with .exe, .bat, .com, .shs, .vbs or .scr, you're definitely looking at a program. If it ends with something else, it might be a program file. In other words, sometimes you can be sure you're dealing with a program, but you can never be sure you aren't – so treat everything with caution!

Most viruses are spread by email (see page 138).

Macro viruses

Some data files can contain macros – small fragments of program code that are used to automate common procedures. For example, an Excel worksheet might include a macro that displays a dialog box when someone tries to enter data. Rather than keying numbers directly into the worksheet, they type them into the dialog box, which provides hints and tips to help them get everything in the right place.

Since macros are basically small programs, they can contain viruses. Macro viruses are a particularly sneaky development, because the files they infect don't look like programs – they look like normal word-processor or spreadsheet data files. Macro viruses are most commonly found in Microsoft Word or Excel documents, although they can infect files from other programs. They've become very common in recent years and even documents from reputable sources may be infected.

Inoculate your computer

Antivirus programs check all the files you download, looking for known viruses and warning you about them. They also make periodic sweeps of your hard disk.

Virus checkers work well as long as you remember three things:

You'll probably have to pay an annual fee to get new versions of the database for your antivirus program.

Be choosy about the sites you download from. Stick to large, well-managed file libraries or get software directly from the company that created it. It's also a good idea to make regular backups of files that contain important data.

- The virus checker has to be running to detect a virus. Most programs run automatically each time you turn on your computer, then lurk in the background, checking every file that you save, copy or download.

- Virus checkers rely on a database that contains details of all the known viruses. If your database is out of date, you may "catch" a new virus that the program doesn't recognize. Companies that produce antivirus software usually let you download the latest version of the database from their Web site. Some programs do this automatically; others require you to get the update yourself. Whatever the procedure, make sure your database is up to date.

- To give your virus checker the best possible chance of detecting a virus, always save suspect files on to your hard disk. Never open program files, Word documents or Excel sheets from within Internet Explorer or Outlook Express.

Virus checkers detect macro viruses as well as the regular sort. Recent versions of Word and Excel can also protect you against these pests. Consult the Help file to find out how to use this feature. If you're using a very old version that doesn't have macro virus protection, use a virus checker on any Word or Excel files before you open them.

Are you being watched?

Spyware is the latest big, bad thing to bedevil the Internet. Spyware programs are designed to collect personal information and transmit it to advertisers and other interested parties. These programs can track your movements on the Web, record the keystrokes you use when entering passwords and even hijack your computer for their own purposes. Related menaces include adware, which is software designed to download and display adverts on your computer.

How did it get on to my computer?

Spyware can also be used for straightforward spying. For example, there are programs that enable companies to monitor their employees and find out whether they're doing legitimate work or using their computers for personal email and online chat.

Spyware is often bundled with other programs. For example, when you install program A, you may also unwittingly install program B, a spyware utility. You think you're getting free software, but there's a price attached – the author is taking your personal information in return. They may sell your browsing details to marketing companies, who can use it to target their advertising, or they may capture your bank account and credit card details and help themselves to your cash.

Spyware programs can also be installed if you're careless about clicking buttons in pop-up windows – separate browser windows that "pop up" when you visit many Web sites. Most pop-up windows contain legitimate adverts, but they can also be used to induce you to install software. For example, clicking a button that says "Close this window" may actually trigger the download and installation of a spyware program.

You can avoid most spyware by following a few simple rules:

- Think twice before you install anything. Do you really need it? Did it come from a reputable source? Stick with software from companies you know, or which has been reviewed and recommended by publications you trust.

- Don't install file-sharing software, such as programs that enable you to exchange music files with other Internet users. These programs are notorious for installing spyware. You may also receive spyware when you exchange files.

- If a dialog box appears on your screen while you're browsing the Web, don't just click the OK button. You should only agree to install software if you know what it does and you trust the company that produced it.

- Use the Pop-up Blocker (see opposite). If you choose to view pop-ups, always close them by clicking the red cross in the top-right corner, or – especially if you're suspicious about the contents – by finding the corresponding button on the Windows taskbar (at the bottom of your screen), right-clicking on it and selecting Close.

- Treat email attachments with suspicion (see page 138)

- Install a firewall such as ZoneAlarm (from Zone Labs at http://www.zonelabs.com/). Firewalls prevent unauthorized programs from accessing the Internet.

Signs that your computer has been infected by spyware include changes to your browser (including new toolbars and changes to your home page), pop-up adverts appearing even when you aren't online and spontaneous activation of your Internet connection. Spyware can also make your computer run more slowly.

There are several programs that detect and remove spyware. If you think you're in need of one, visit Download.com (see page 107). Follow the links to its Spyware Center and read the reviews.

Do you accept cookies from strangers?

Cookies are small text files that Web sites store on your computer. For example, when you first visit a site, it might ask for your name. It then stores that information in a cookie on your hard disk. When you return to that site, it looks in the cookie file, retrieves your name and creates a page that says, "Hello, Mary".

Cookies are used to record your preferences and customize Web sites accordingly. Most are completely innocent. However, they can also be used to track your browsing and record which adverts you've seen, so marketing companies can target you more accurately.

For more details about different types of cookies and their possible functions, go to Help>Contents and Index and click the Index tab. Type "cookies" into the keyword box.

You can decide whether to accept cookies:

1 Run Internet Explorer and go to Tools>Internet Options

2 Click the Privacy tab. Adjust the slider upwards (to accept fewer cookies) or downwards (to accept more cookies)

Pesky pop-ups

Even when they aren't vehicles for spyware, pop-up windows can be annoying. Sometimes they provide helpful information, such as a menu or instructions for navigating a Web site. However, most of the time they are used to display adverts. Some sites spawn pop-up windows relentlessly, opening a replacement window each time you close one down. Others hide their pop-up adverts under the main window, so you don't find them until you close Internet Explorer (these windows are called "pop unders").

Pop-ups can be useful, but the majority are not

The Pop-up Blocker is only available in the version of Internet Explorer supplied with Windows XP SP2 (see page 23 for details about upgrading).

Internet Explorer blocks most pop-up windows, allowing only the ones that are triggered when you click on a link or button (for example, to bring up a second window that explains how to use an online shopping site). This feature is normally turned on.

> When a Web site tries to create a pop-up window automatically, Internet Explorer blocks the pop-up. It makes a "blip blip" sound and displays the yellow Information bar

Selecting Temporarily Allow Pop-ups doesn't always work. This is because some pop-ups are designed to only appear once. If they are squelched by the Pop-up Blocker, they won't appear again, even though you've told Internet Explorer to display them. You may be able to coax them out of hiding by turning off the Pop-up Blocker, closing Internet Explorer, reopening it and returning to the site.

2 To see the pop-up window, click on the Information bar and select Temporarily Allow Pop-ups. The pop-up window should appear

3 If you visit this site regularly and want to allow it to create pop-ups, click Always Allow Pop-ups from This Site…, then click Yes

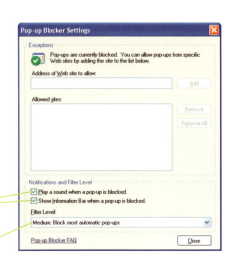

4 To turn off the Pop-up Blocker, go to Tools>Pop-up Blocker> Turn Off Pop-up Blocker. To turn it back on, go to Tools> Pop-up Blocker>Turn On Pop-up Blocker

5 To change the settings, go to Tools>Pop-up Blocker>Pop-up Blocker Settings…

6 Turn off the sound and/or Information bar warning by deselecting these checkboxes

7 Set the Filter Level to High to block all pop-ups

Other security problems

Back in Chapter 5 you installed several add-on programs so you could enjoy multimedia files such as sounds and videos. You also learned that Web pages can contain scripts – fragments of program code that add interactive elements. Both these technologies could potentially be abused to cause problems for your computer. On the other hand, they help make Web sites dynamic and interesting.

The security settings complement the activities of your virus checker.

They can help you avoid problems a virus checker might miss, but they don't protect you from viruses.

Internet Explorer provides four security settings – High, Medium, Medium-Low and Low – that enable you to trade off excitement against security when you're browsing the Web. The settings cover all kinds of interactive content, file downloads and communication with insecure sites (see page 96).

- **High** prevents you from downloading anything that could cause problems, keeping you safe but cutting you off from some of the more exciting aspects of the Web.

- **Medium** is less severe: it bans some unsafe content and warns you about the rest.

- **Medium-Low** is the same, but without the warnings.

- The **Low** setting provides hardly any protection.

1 Go to Tools>Internet Options, then click the Security tab

The Local Intranet zone contains the computers on a local computer network, such as a company's internal network. The Trusted Sites and Restricted Sites zones can be customized to include sites you feel good or bad about. You can use a different setting for each zone, if you're so inclined. However, the Internet zone is the important one.

2 Choose the Internet zone

3 Move the slider to High (at the top) to eliminate potential hazards

4 Medium security exposes you to some risks, but enables you to enjoy interactive Web content. You are warned about potential hazards

5 Don't use the Medium-Low or Low settings for general browsing

File Transfer Protocol

This chapter has focused on downloading program files with a Web browser, because that's what most people do. It isn't the most efficient approach, but it's easy and convenient, and perfectly adequate if you don't download files very often.

In the days before Web browsers, people used a different system known as File Transfer Protocol (FTP). As you might expect from the name, it was entirely about transferring files and no use for anything else.

You can still use File Transfer Protocol today. All you need is an FTP program, such as GlobalSCAPE's CuteFTP or Ipswitch's WS_FTP. Find out more and/or obtain copies of these programs from the following Web sites:

GlobalSCAPE, at: http://www.cuteftp.com/
Ipswitch Software, at: http://www.ipswitch.com/

FTP programs show the files on your computer on one side of the screen and the files from a computer on the Internet on the other side. To move a file from one computer to the other, you simply select it and click a button or drag it across with the mouse.

Your files and folders

Files and folders on

remote computer

You may want to learn more about FTP if you decide to create your own Web site (see Chapter 12), because it makes it easy to upload your pages.

Send me an email

Electronic mail is quick, quiet, cheap, convenient, courteous… and easy to send and receive. What more could you want? Find out how it works, how to keep your addresses and messages in order, and how to sidestep viruses and junk mail.

Covers

Chapter Eight

E is for email

Email is short for electronic mail, the Internet equivalent of letters and faxes. However, it's better than both of those:

- **Email is quick.** It only takes a couple of minutes to send a message to someone, no matter where in the world they are. A letter might take days or even weeks.

- **Email is cheap.** Even if you pay for your connection by the minute, you won't run up a significant bill sending emails, because all the time-consuming activities take place offline. You only have to be connected to the Internet when you're sending or receiving messages. You can read your mail and write replies after you have disconnected.

- **Email is convenient.** You don't need to find an envelope, buy a stamp or look for a mail box. You can do everything from home, at any hour of the day.

Email is great for queries with straightforward answers. If you need to discuss something, it's better to use the telephone. Don't try to carry out complex negotiations by email.

- **It helps you stay in touch.** Email is great for contacting people who are perpetually on the phone or out of the office. Instead of spending half the day playing telephone tag, you can email your queries and comments and let them respond when they can. It also makes it easier to deal with people in different time zones. Sending an email is more considerate than calling at an awkward hour.

- **You can send people files.** You can attach text documents, pictures, sound clips and program files to your messages. If you're collaborating on a project, you can send people editable documents instead of expecting them to re-enter information from a letter or fax. It's also a great way to share holiday snaps and family photographs.

- **You can do mass mailings.** Printing newsletters and mailing them out to customers or club members can be expensive and time consuming. With email, you simply compose a message and send it to everyone on your mailing list. It's a great way to inform people about special offers and upcoming events.

To send an email to someone, you just need to know their address, which will look something like:

joe@someservice.com

| The part before the @ is the recipient's name or user name | The part after the @ is the address of the recipient's company or service provider |

When you send an email message, it crosses the Internet very quickly. If the recipient's computer is permanently connected to the Internet, for example via a company network, it reaches them in a couple of minutes.

If the recipient uses a modem to connect to the Internet, your message is delivered to their service provider. It is deposited in their mail box and waits there until they log on and check for new email. It's like sending a letter to someone with a post-office box: they don't know your message is there until they go to the post office and open their mail box. Most people check their mail at least once a day, but some people only log on occasionally – in which case it may be a while before you get a reply.

Choose a mail program

 You can also sign up for a Web-based email service and send and receive email using your Web browser – see Chapter 9.

You need an email program to send and receive email messages. Most programs have four basic functions:

- They let you compose messages in a word processor-style window. Usually you can add formatting and insert pictures.

- They dispatch your messages and check your mail box for incoming mail.

- They enable you to read and file the messages you receive.

- They store the addresses of the people you correspond with.

Popular email programs include Microsoft's Outlook Express (included in Windows) and its big brother Outlook (supplied with Microsoft Office), along with Mozilla's Thunderbird and Qualcomm's Eudora. All these programs enable you to send messages to any Internet user, including people with other email programs. You only need to have the same email program as your friends if you want to send messages with complicated formatting.

Eudora can display messages created with Outlook Express, and vice versa

This book concentrates on Outlook Express. It was designed as a companion program for Internet Explorer and is included with Windows, so it's a good choice for beginners. For information about the alternatives, visit the following Web sites:

Mozilla, at: http://www.mozilla.org/
Qualcomm, at: http://www.eudora.com/

Introducing Outlook Express

Outlook Express isn't just an email program; you can also use it to access Usenet newsgroups (see Chapter 10). It has quite a lot in common with Outlook, the mail program supplied with Microsoft Office, but it's more specialized. Outlook Express is optimized for sending mail over the Internet, whereas Outlook also has features for communicating with coworkers over a company network.

1 To run Outlook Express, click the Start button and select it from the left-hand side of the Start menu

If you used a CD from your service provider to configure your Internet connection (see page 34), you've probably set up your account already.

2 The first time you do this, you may be prompted to fill in the details of your email account. You'll need to know your email address and the addresses of your service provider's mail servers (if you don't have this information, call your service provider)

3 Enter your name

4 Click Next to continue (and again after each step)

5 Enter your email address

6 Enter the addresses of your service provider's mail servers

When you collect email, you have to send your user name and password twice: once to connect to your service provider and again to access your mail box. Windows XP can automate both log-ins.

7 Fill in your user name and password. Usually these are the same as the ones you use to connect to the Internet (see page 34), but some service providers give you a separate user name and/or password for email

8 Click Finish

Make yourself at home

The Outlook Express window is divided into several panes:

Folder list – folders for
all your messages

Toolbar

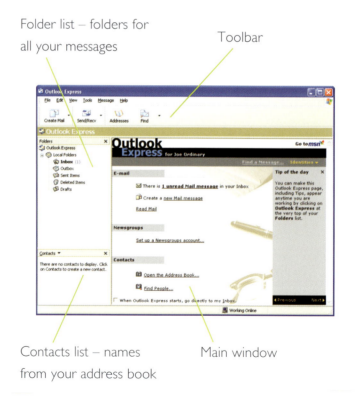

Contacts list – names
from your address book

Main window

1 Select Inbox from the folder list to open your Inbox. The main window is divided in two:

Message list – lists all the messages in this folder

Preview pane – displays the selected message

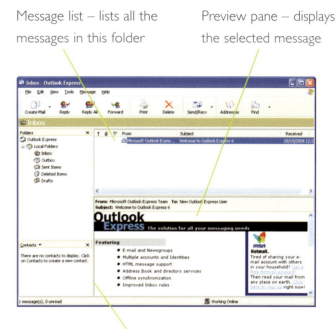

2 Drag the gray dividing bars to adjust the relative sizes of the panes

3 To make further changes, go to View>Layout

It's a good idea to turn off the preview pane. If you leave it on, Outlook Express automatically displays the latest message each time you download your mail. Some viruses can be caught by previewing a message – see page 138.

4 Select the items you want to display

5 Click Customize Toolbar to add or remove toolbar buttons, change the button size or hide the text labels

Send an email

You have to be connected to the Internet to send a message, but you don't have to be online while you compose it. It's best to write your messages before you log on, then send them all in a batch. You can collect any new messages at the same time (see opposite).

1   To write a message, click the Create Mail button, select File>New>Mail Message or press Ctrl+N

2   A New Message window appears

If you have Microsoft Office on your PC, you can spell-check your message. Click the Spelling button, select Tools>Spelling or press F7.

3   Enter the email address of the recipient

4   Fill in the Subject: line

5   Compose your message

To determine whether Outlook Express sends messages immediately, go to Tools>Options and click the Send tab. If "Send messages immediately" is selected, it sends each message as soon as you click the Send button. If you use a modem to connect to the Internet, deselect that option. You can then collect messages in your Outbox and send them in batches. You may prefer this option even if you have a broadband connection, because it gives you a chance to think about your messages before you send them.

6   Click the Send button or press Alt+S. If Outlook Express is set up to send messages immediately, it dispatches the message

7   If Outlook Express is not set up to send messages immediately, it transfers the message to the Outbox

8   When you're ready to send the messages in your Outbox, click the Send/Recv button or press Ctrl+M.

Outlook Express connects to the Internet and dispatches them

Receive messages

Unlike "real" mail, email messages aren't delivered to your door – or in this case, computer. When someone sends you an email, it's delivered to your service provider's mail server, which puts it into your personal mail box. You must then log on and collect it.

1 To check your mail box, click Send/Recv. Outlook Express connects to the Internet (if necessary), sends any messages waiting in your Outbox and fetches any new mail. The new messages are placed in your Inbox. You can log off and read them in your own time

2 Select the Inbox folder to see the messages you have received

3 Double-click on a message to display it in a separate window

Reply and forward

It's easy to reply to an email message, because Outlook Express automatically adds the correct address.

1 To reply to a message, click on its entry in the message list to select it. Click the Reply button, select Message>Reply to Sender or press Ctrl+R. Outlook Express opens a New Message window

2 The To: and Subject: lines are already filled in

3 The text from the previous message is quoted at the bottom

4 Type your reply

5 Delete any superfluous material from the bottom section, then send the message as usual

Forwarding messages

You can also divert an email message to a friend or to someone who is better able to respond to the sender.

1 To forward a message, select it and click the Forward button. Alternatively, select Message> Forward or press Ctrl+F. Enter the new address in the To: line

2 Add any comments you wish to make above the quoted text, then send the message

Address book

The Address Book enables you to store all the email addresses you use regularly. You can then add them to messages more easily.

1   To open the Address Book, click the Addresses button, select Tools>Address Book or press Ctrl+Shift+B

Addresses

It's even easier to add the address of someone who has sent you a message. Select the message, then go to Tools> Add Sender to Address Book.

Outlook Express may automatically add people you reply to. To turn this option on or off, go to Tools>Options and click the Send tab.

2   To add an address, click the New button and select New Contact. You can also select File>New Contact or press Ctrl+N

3   Fill in the person's name and (optionally) nickname

4   Enter their email address and click Add. Repeat if they have several

5   Click the Home, Business, Personal and Other tabs to add any extra information you wish to record. Click OK to finish

To access the Address Book from the New Message window, click the address book icon 📖 at the left of the To: line.

6   You can now enter the person's name or nickname in the To: line of your messages. Outlook Express looks up the address when you send the message. Alternatively, double-click the person's entry in the Contacts list to create a pre-addressed message form

Organize your messages

Initially you have five email folders: Inbox, Outbox, Sent Items, Deleted Items and Drafts.

- New email is deposited in the Inbox (see page 127).

- Outgoing email waits in the Outbox (see page 126).

- Once a message has been dispatched, it is moved to the Sent Items folder so you have a copy.

The Deleted Items folder is like the Windows Recycle Bin – it stores items you think you won't need again until you're ready to get rid of them for good. To empty the folder, select Edit>Empty 'Deleted Items' Folder.

- If you select a message and click Delete, select Edit> Delete, press Delete or press Ctrl+D, it ends up in the Deleted Items folder. You can rescue it if necessary.

- If you close a message without sending it, Outlook Express asks if you want to save the changes. Click Yes to move the message to the Drafts folder so you can finish it later on.

Sort your email

As well as placing your email in these folders, Outlook Express enables you to sort the messages in each one.

A small gray arrow within the tab tells you which column is being used to sort the messages. It points upwards for a regular sort and downwards for a reverse sort.

To change the column headings, right-click on one of the tabs and select Columns…

To sort your messages, click one of the gray tabs at the top of the list. Click again to reverse the sort

Sorted by date

Sorted by sender

Create your own folders

Some messages can be deleted as soon as you've read them, but there'll be others you want to keep. Create extra email folders and file them away tidily.

1 To create a new email folder, go to File>Folder>New

2 Enter a name

3 To create a new top-level folder, select Local Folders. To add a subfolder, select one of your existing folders

If the folder ends up in the wrong place, use the mouse to drag it around the Folder list.

4 Click OK to add the folder to the Folder list

If you can't remember where you filed an important message, click the Find button, go to Edit>Find>Message or press Ctrl+Shift+F. You can search by subject or sender, or look for messages that contain a word or phrase.

5 Use the mouse to drag messages into the new folder. You can also select them (hold down Shift or Ctrl to select several at once), then go to Edit>Move to Folder. Select the folder and click OK

Formatted email

Outlook Express enables you to format your email messages so they are as attractive as Web pages (the formatting is added using HTML, the language used to create Web pages).

Formatted mail is fun and can be useful when you're trying to catch someone's eye. However, it's only a good idea if you're sure the other person uses a program that can handle HTML mail. Formatted messages look awful in older email programs and some people find them irritating. If in doubt, stick to plain text.

1   Use the New Message window's Format menu to switch between Rich Text (HTML) and Plain Text. A formatting bar appears when Rich Text is selected

Stick to fonts that the other person is likely to have: Arial, Comic Sans, Georgia, Impact, Times New Roman, Trebuchet and Verdana.

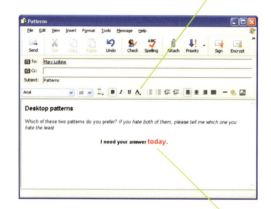

2   Use the drop-down lists and buttons to format your text

The picture must be saved in the .gif or .jpg format.

3   To add a picture, click Insert Picture 🖼 or select Insert> Picture. Click Browse and locate the picture file. Click OK

4   To add a horizontal line, click Insert Horizontal Line ▬ or select Insert>Horizontal Line

Don't feel obliged to format your messages. Experienced Internet users regard email as a fast and easy way to communicate and prefer to receive quick notes in Plain Text format.

You can tell Outlook Express to use Plain Text by default. Go to Tools>Options and click the Send tab. Under "Mail Sending Format", select "Plain Text".

5 To create a fancy backdrop, go to Format>Background. Select Color for a solid color or Picture to insert an image

6 If you're inserting an image, click Browse to locate the file, then click OK

7 The image appears behind your text

Where are my pictures?

When you receive a formatted message, Outlook Express may not display the pictures. This is because junk mail (see page 141) can contain pictures that act as signalling beacons, enabling the sender of the message to confirm that your address is valid.

1 When Outlook Express blocks pictures, it displays a warning message below the subject line

2 If you trust the sender, click the warning message to download and display the pictures

Stationery

Outlook Express comes with predesigned Stationery that can add a touch of class to your correspondence or help you celebrate special occasions. However, Stationery is formatted mail (the fact that it was formatted by someone else makes no difference), so it's only a good idea if you're sure the recipient can display it.

To specify a default Stationery design, go to Tools>Options. Click the Compose tab, select "Mail:" and pick a design.

1 To compose a new email message using Stationery, click the arrow next to the Create Mail button and select a design

2 The menu only lists a few of the designs. Click Select Stationery for more choices

To design your own Stationery, go to Tools> Options and click the Compose tab. Click the Create New button to run the Stationery Wizard.

There's also a Download More button that takes you to Microsoft's Web site, where you'll find lots of extra designs.

3 Complete and send your message as usual. You can add additional formatting if you wish

4 You can also add stationery to a message that you're halfway through composing. Make sure Rich Text format is selected (see page 132), then go to Format>Apply Stationery

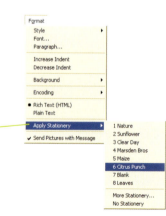

Signatures

A signature is a short piece of text that is appended to the end of every message you send. If you're sending messages from work, it could include your contact details. For personal messages, you might use a catch phrase or favorite quote. Keep it short, though – long signatures soon become tiresome.

You can create several signatures. You might use different ones for business and personal messages. However, you'll have to sign your messages manually – see below.

1 Go to Tools>Options and click the Signatures tab

2 Click New

3 Click Rename and give the signature a sensible name

4 Select "Text" and enter the text you want to add to your messages

If you only want to sign some of your messages, don't select "Add…". Instead, use the Insert>Signature menu option to add your signature manually before you send your messages.

5 If you want to sign all your messages, select the "Add signatures to all outgoing messages" option at the top of the dialog box

6 Click OK

7 The signature text is added to the end of every message you create

Attachments

You can email pictures, document files and programs to friends and family. If you have a digital camera or microphone, you can bring your messages to life with snapshots or recordings. More prosaically, being able to exchange files by email is handy when you're working from home.

1 Compose your message (see page 126) and click the Attach button. Alternatively, select File Attachment from the New Message window's Insert menu

You can attach any kind of file, but don't send your friends large files without warning them first. Make sure they have the right software for viewing your files.

2 Find the file(s) you want to send – you can select several files at once by holding down Shift or Ctrl

3 Click Attach

If you change your mind about one of the files, right-click on its entry in the Attach: line, then select Remove from the pop-up menu.

4 The files are added to the message

5 Send the message in the usual way

...cont'd

If you receive a file from someone you don't know, don't open it. The safest option is to delete the entire message. Alternatively, save the file on to your hard disk and check for viruses before you open it. This also applies to Word and Excel documents, which can carry macro viruses (see page 111).

Receiving attachments

When you receive a message with attached files, you have two main choices: open the files or save them on to your hard disk. It is usually better to save them.

1 If you see a paper-clip icon in the message list, the associated message has one or more files attached

2 When you open the message, the attached files are listed at the top. In some cases – for example, when a .gif or .jpg image has been attached – the file is displayed at the end of the text

Outlook Express normally prevents you from opening and saving potentially dangerous program files. If you really, really need to receive a program file by email, you can turn this feature off. Go to Tools>Options and click the Security tab, then deselect "Do not allow attachments to be saved..." In general, though, it's a much better idea to keep this option selected and take delivery of the program file by some other means.

3 Right-click on a file to open it or save it. You can also save all the attached files at once

4 Click Browse and choose a folder

5 Select the files you want to save and click Save

Viruses by email

Viruses are designed to spread themselves as widely as possible. The malicious programmers who produce viruses want to get their creations on to as many computers as possible, as quickly as possible. Over the last few years they've figured out how to harness the power of email to distribute viruses. You are almost certain to receive an infected email at some point, so you should learn how to recognize a problem and protect your computer.

There are several things you should know about viruses that are transmitted by email:

People used to tell beginners they couldn't catch a virus simply by opening an email message. With the advent of formatted mail, that's no longer true.

- Most viruses travel as attachments. However, there are some that hide themselves in the body of a formatted message. You can catch this type of virus simply by previewing or opening the infected message.

- If a friend or coworker picks up a virus, they may pass it on unwittingly. The virus may secretly attach itself to every message they send, or go through their address book and send fake messages to everyone they know. Each message carries a copy of the virus.

- Some viruses can fake (or "spoof") the From: address in the emails they send out. Suppose you have two friends, Joe and Tina, and Joe catches the Klez virus. It goes through his computer, looking for email addresses, and finds Tina's address. It then creates a fake message that appears to be from Tina and sends it to you. You are running a virus checker (of course) and it sounds the alarm. Since the message came from Tina, you tell her to check her computer, but she says she doesn't have the virus. She is right – it is Joe's computer that is sending out the messages. You can even receive an infected message that appears to have come from your own computer.

- Some viruses also attach random files from your computer to the messages they send out. This can be embarrassing if they choose confidential documents.

Keep your computer healthy

Avoiding viruses is mostly a matter of common sense:

- Run a virus checker and keep its database up to date (see page 112). Make sure it is set up to check email messages as well as files that you download or copy on to your hard disk.

- Turn off Outlook Express' Preview pane (see page 125).

- Check that Outlook Express is using a high level of security when opening messages. To do this, run Internet Explorer and go to Tools>Internet Options. Click the Security tab, then select the Restricted Sites zone. Make sure its security level is set to High (see page 117). Click OK, then switch to Outlook Express. Select Tools>Options and click the Security tab. Under "Virus Protection", set "Select the Internet Explorer security zone to use" to "Restricted sites zone (More secure)".

This trick is useful when you get a message that sounds legitimate. For example, if you've sent a query to an online shop, you may not recognize the name of the person who replies. By checking the Properties box, you can at least find out whether they work for the company you've been communicating with.

- Don't open email messages from strangers – delete them. If you aren't sure whether a message is legitimate, right-click on its entry in the message list and select Properties. You can then see the sender's email address, which may include the name of their company.

- Be suspicious if a friend sends you a message with an unusual or unlikely subject, especially if it has attached files. Give them a ring and see if they actually sent the message.

- Set up your computer to display file extensions (see page 74) and learn to recognize the dangerous ones (see page 111). Watch out for double extensions, such as picture.gif.exe. It's the letters at the end (in this case, .exe) that count.

Sooner or later you will receive a virus from one of your friends. Don't let your guard down just because you know the person who sent the message.

- Always save attached files on to your hard disk before you open them. Saving the files gives your virus checker a second chance to inspect them.

- Don't yell at your friend when they send you viruses. They may have done so unwittingly, or the virus may have come from somewhere else. Concentrate on finding the source and stamping out the infection.

Virus hoaxes

There are a number of virus hoaxes that do the rounds by email. The classic example is a message that tells you not to open messages with "Good Times" in the subject line. Doing so will delete your files and destroy your processor – or so the story goes.

The warning is a hoax and the virus it describes does not exist. However, the Good Times email is almost as troublesome as a real virus, because people waste a lot of time forwarding the message to their friends, calling their systems manager and so on.

If you receive a warning that might be a hoax, don't pass it on "just in case". You'll get your less knowledgeable friends worried over nothing. Those with more experience will sigh deeply as they delete your message.

How can you tell whether a virus warning is a hoax? Be suspicious of any warning message that:

- Contains lots of exclamation marks!!!!!

- Tells you something dreadful will happen if you open an email message with a particular title.

- Promises total destruction of your hard disk, your processor, your entire computer, your home…

- References a technical-sounding organization you've never heard of and can't find on the Web.

- Encourages you to pass it on to all your friends.

You can find out whether your message is a well-known hoax by looking it up on one of the following Web sites:

CIAC Internet Hoaxes, at: http://hoaxbusters.ciac.org/
Symantec Security Response, at: http://www.symantec.com/avcenter/

Junk mail

The ease with which you can send email or create Web pages encourages some people to abuse these services. You shouldn't believe everything you read on the Web and you shouldn't take every email message seriously.

Platefuls of spam

Unsolicited commercial email is known as "spam" (after a Monty Python sketch set in café where every dish contains spam). You can expect to receive messages offering you miracle cures, better credit ratings, improvements to your sex life, x-rated pictures, vinyl siding for your house (?!) and so on.

Spam is annoying but hard to avoid – it's a fact of Internet life

If you notice that you are getting a lot of messages from a particular address, select the next one, then go to Tools>Block Sender. Future messages from that person will be consigned to the bin.

There's very little you can do about junk mail. There are anti-spam programs that try to filter it out, but they don't always get it right. Otherwise the best option is to delete it, unopened.

Some junk mails claim that if you reply to a particular address, or reply with "remove" in the Subject: line, your name will be taken off the mailing list. Don't bother doing this – the company just wants to confirm that their messages are getting through.

Chain letters

There are two sorts of chain letters. One type has a list of names and promises you enormous wealth if you send a small sum of money to the person at the top. You're then supposed to add your name and redistribute the message. It's mathematically impossible for most of these schemes to pay off and they're probably illegal.

Many service providers will close your account if they catch you forwarding this kind of junk.

The other type promises you good luck if you forward it to all your friends and bad luck if you don't. Some of these messages are very unpleasant and you should delete them. You aren't doing your friends any favors by sending them messages that threaten all sorts of dire consequences if they "break the chain".

The Craig Shergold story is an urban legend – a tale that keeps being told, regardless of its veracity. You can find many more in the Urban Legends Reference Pages, at: http://www.snopes.com/

You may also receive chain letters that ask you to send cards to a sick child – usually Craig Shergold, a boy with cancer – who is trying to get into *The Guinness Book of Records*. There's some truth to this story, which dates back to the late 1980s. However, Shergold got his record a long time ago. He also had an operation and recovered. He would really like people to stop sending cards.

Scams and frauds

There are numerous scams circulating the Internet, some of which are quite convincing. Be suspicious of anything that sounds too good to be true and learn to recognize the most common tricks.

Many different tsunami scams appeared within hours of the earthquake and tsunami that struck the Indian Ocean on 26 December 2004. Always make sure you are dealing with a legitimate organization and don't let your compassion overrule your common sense.

One of the most serious scams is the Nigerian Advance Fee scam (also known as the 419 fraud). Victims receive a message purportedly from someone in Nigeria (or a similar country). The sender claims they have access to a large sum of money and need help to get it out of Nigeria. If the victim helps the writer, they'll receive a share of the profits.

Once a victim is hooked, the writer starts to request money – for example, to bribe government officials. Victims are also encouraged to travel to Nigeria or a neutral country to complete the deal. They may then be threatened with violence, held hostage or murdered.

For more information about this scam and many others, visit Internet ScamBusters, at: http://www.scambusters.org/

Mail on the move

Off to see the world… or making a trip to Hicksville, home of your company's head office? Either way, Web-based mail services enable you to collect your messages from any computer with an Internet connection.

Covers

Chapter Nine

Web-based mail

Web-based mail systems enable you to send and receive messages from any computer that's connected to the Internet, using a Web browser. You can check your mail using a computer at work, at a friend's place or in a cybercafé, without having to set up an email program or enter lots of personal details.

You can access a Hotmail account from anywhere

Web-based mail is great when you're traveling. Instead of lugging around a laptop or making expensive phone calls, you can stay in touch by popping into cybercafés or using computers in public places such as libraries and airports. Your friends and relatives can always contact you, without needing to know where you are, and you can send them a day-by-day account of your adventures.

Web-based mail is also useful when you want to send personal messages from a company computer. Some organizations frown on people using company facilities for personal correspondence. They may not want people to mistake you for a company spokesperson. Also, you may want to keep some of your correspondence private. Your systems administrator can intercept any messages you send through your company's mail server, which can be embarrassing when you're applying for another job (they may also monitor your Web usage, so for real privacy, use the Internet from home).

The downside of Web-based mail systems is that you have to be connected to the Internet to read or write messages. If you're only going to be sending email from home, it's better to use a regular mail service. You'll spend less time online and you'll be able to take advantage of the extra features of a dedicated email program such as Outlook Express.

Choose a mail service

There are thousands of Web-based mail services and most of them offer free accounts. Popular services include:

Hotmail, at: http://www.hotmail.com/
Mail.com, at: http://www.mail.com/
Yahoo! Mail, at: http://mail.yahoo.com/

There are also many smaller services that offer amusing addresses such as joe@madmanmail.com or tina@tough.com

When you're choosing a Web-based mail service, keep the following points in mind:

- **Will it still be operating a year from now?** Internet businesses come and go at an alarming rate. Choosing a service that's supported by a large company increases your chances of an enduring relationship.

- **If the service is free, how is it funded?** Many services add a tag line to every message you send, promoting themselves to all your contacts. You might not find that acceptable for business mail. Most services display adverts on their Web pages and some sell your details to marketing companies.

- **What addresses are available?** Can you have something simple, or will you be joe567542@someplace.com?

- **What do you get?** How much space will you have for storing messages? Can you set up an address book? Can you attach files to your messages? Is there a spell-checker?

- **What options are available?** Some companies offer a fairly basic free service, then give you the option to pay for extras such as removal of the adverts, more storage space or access to your messages from a regular email program.

Regular email services are often described as "POP3" mail services. The acronym is short for Post Office Protocol 3, the normal method for receiving messages via a mail box (see page 127).

Open an account

Once you've chosen a Web-based mail service, opening an account is straightforward. Choose a user name and password, enter some personal details and you're in business.

Suppose you've decided to open a Yahoo! Mail account:

1 Visit the Yahoo! Mail Web site at: http://mail.yahoo.com/ and follow the links to sign up for a new account. You can open a free account or pay for extra features

2 Choose an ID (you can only use letters, numbers and underlines) and password. Answer the security question and fill in your personal details

3 Read the Terms of Service. Click I Agree to accept the rules and create your email account

4 You'll then be
taken to your
online mail box

5 When you return to the Yahoo! Mail site, enter your user name
and password to sign in and access your mail

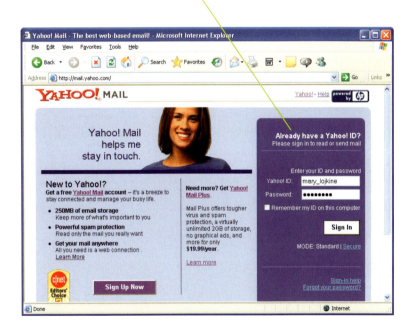

Read your mail

You can read your mail from any computer with a Web browser and an Internet connection.

1 Go to the Yahoo! Mail site and log in to your account

2 Select the Inbox to view your messages

3 Click one of the messages

4 The message is displayed

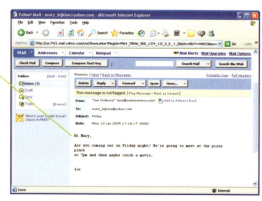

Send a message

Sending messages is equally straightforward. Yahoo! Mail lets you format your messages, add clickable Web links and attach files from your hard disk.

1 Log on to Yahoo! Mail. To create a new message, click Compose. To reply to an existing one, open it and click Reply

2 Enter the address and subject

To add a clickable link, select the text you want to link from, then click the Create Hyperlink ⬛ button. Fill in the address of the page you want to link to.

3 Compose your message

4 To send files with your message, click Attach Files

5 Click the Browse button(s) and find the file(s) on your hard disk. Click Attach Files

6 The files are added to the message

7 Click the Send button to dispatch your message

Use the Address Book

The Address Book stores the addresses of people you write to regularly, so you don't have to type them in each time.

You can also open a message and click the "Add to Address Book" link.

1 To add someone to your Address Book, click Addresses. Select the "Add a New Contact" option or click Add Contact

2 Fill in their details and click Save

If you can't remember someone's nickname, click the "Insert Addresses" link to access your complete Address Book.

3 The next time you want to send a message to this person enter their nickname. Yahoo Mail displays the matching addresses

4 Click the address you want to use

Make friends online

Even with millions of people online, the Internet can be a lonely place. This chapter explains how to use message boards and newsgroups to meet people who share your interests. Fire out a few opinions and you'll soon be making friends.

Covers

Chapter Ten

Where are all the people?

At any time of the day, there are millions of people using the Internet, but it hardly ever feels crowded. You don't get elbowed by a passing stranger or pushed out of the way and you don't have to queue. Sometimes it feels as if you have the whole World Wide Web to yourself, which is great… but also lonely.

If you want to meet Internet users who share your interests, stop browsing and start interacting. Get involved in message boards and newsgroups, where you can share your thoughts and opinions. You'll soon come across people who agree (or disagree) with your point of view and before long you'll be having free and frank exchanges on all sorts of subjects. It's a great way to make friends.

Leave a message

Message boards enable you to express your opinions via the Web.

Some message boards function like the letters pages of a newspaper. The Webmaster asks a question or proposes a topic and visitors add their remarks. For example, the BBC News Web site has a "Have Your Say" area where you can comment on the issues of the day.

Message boards are also known as forums.

Other message boards are more conversational. Someone makes a comment, someone else replies, a third person adds something, and the original person responds to the points raised. Most boards confine themselves to a single topic. For example, there are message boards dedicated to scuba diving, photography, movies and, of course, computers.

Did you hear the news?

Usenet newsgroups are completely separate from the Web. They were created to enable Internet users to exchange gossip, trivia, advice, insults and – very occasionally – news.

You can think of a newsgroup as a public mail box for messages on a particular topic. Anyone can post a comment, and anyone else can read it and upload a reply.

The name Usenet is derived from "User Network". Usenet is a network of computers (news servers) that store news messages.

Unlike Web pages, newsgroups aren't stored in a specific place. All the messages are copied from one news server to the next, so you don't have to connect to lots of different sites. You just download the latest messages from your service provider's news server.

alt.who.what.where?

There are over 50,000 newsgroups, although some service providers only carry the more popular ones. Each newsgroup is dedicated to a different topic and its name tells you what to expect. For example, there's a newsgroup called:

rec.arts.movies.reviews

Each section of the name reduces the scope. In this case rec stands for recreation, arts and movies are self-evident and the group only carries reviews. There are a dozen other movies groups, 100 other arts groups, and over 600 rec groups in total.

rec is only one of dozens of top-level categories. Other important categories include:

There are also newsgroup hierarchies for different countries. There are lots of UK groups, for example. You'll also come across groups for people from Australia (aus), New Zealand (nz), South Africa (za), Singapore (sg) and many other places.

- **Alternative** (alt). The alt hierarchy is one of the liveliest sections of Usenet. Some of the groups are pretty wild, but most are just odd. It's also a nursery for new newsgroups.

- **Computing** (comp), for everything from hardware and software to artificial intelligence and home automation.

- **Miscellaneous** (misc). Things that don't fit anywhere else.

- **Usenet** (news), for discussion about Usenet. The news.announce.newusers group has advice for beginners.

- **Recreation** (rec), for hobbies, sports, arts and music. The rec groups are friendlier than the alt groups and it's easy to find your way around, so rec is a good place to start.

- **Science** (sci), for mathematics, physics, engineering, chemistry, biological science, medicine, psychology and philosophy – everything except computing.

- **Social** (soc), for social issues such as culture, religion, politics, history and mental health.

Use a message board

Web-based message boards are easy to use. If you've used Web-based mail (see Chapter 9), you'll find the procedures familiar. The main difference is that your message isn't sent to a specific person. Instead, it is displayed publicly for everyone to read.

If you're interested in scuba diving, Scuba Board is a good place to start. Find it at: http://www.scubaboard.com/

1 Like most message boards, it is divided into forums for various subjects. Select a forum to see the topics under discussion

2 Select a topic to see what people have to say

3 To add your opinion, click Reply

Most message boards allow anyone to read messages. If you want to post replies, you'll probably need to register. You'll have to choose a user name and password and agree to a set of terms and conditions.

4 You may have to register before you can have your say

5 Give your response a title

6 Enter your comments

7 Scroll down and click Submit Reply

8 Your message is added at the bottom of the page

There are lots of other message boards that use similar procedures (often because they use the same software to run the board). To find a message board on a particular subject, use a search engine such as Google (see page 61).

Most message boards are friendly and welcome newcomers. However, it's a good idea to familiarize yourself with the general rules for polite behavior before you start posting messages. See page 161 for information about "Netiquette".

Choose a newsreader

Whereas message boards are part of the Web, newsgroups are completely separate. You'll need a specialized program called a newsgroup reader or newsreader to access them.

Reading and posting newsgroup messages is similar to reading and sending email, so some mail programs – including Outlook Express – can double as newsreaders. This is a good option for beginners because you already have the software and know how to use the basic features.

If you find yourself spending a lot of time reading newsgroups, you might want to use a dedicated newsreader such as Agent (from Forté, at: http://www.forteinc.com/). These programs have extra tools that help you filter out the rubbish and concentrate on the conversations you find interesting.

Agent lists newsgroup names on the left and message titles on the right. Message text appears at the bottom

Find some newsgroups

The rest of this chapter explains how to use Outlook Express to access newsgroups. The first thing you need to do is find out the address of your service provider's news server and set up Outlook Express to connect to it.

1 Run Outlook Express and select Tools>Accounts. Click Add and select News

2 Enter your name and email address, clicking Next after each step

3 Fill in the address of your service provider's news server

4 If you are required to log on, select this box. Click Next and enter your user name and password

5 When you get back to the Internet Accounts dialog box, click the News tab. You should see an entry for your news server. Select it and click the Properties button to give it a sensible name

6 When you click Close, Outlook Express asks if you want to download newsgroups. Click Yes

...cont'd

6 Outlook Express downloads the names of the newsgroups carried by your service provider. This process takes a few minutes, but you only have to do it once

Subscribing to a newsgroup isn't like subscribing to a magazine or joining a club. You don't have to pay and you won't be added to a membership list. Subscribing just tells Outlook Express that you're interested in a newsgroup – it's like making a Favorite for a Web site.

7 The newsgroup list appears. You need to select some newsgroups and "subscribe" to them

8 Scroll down the list until you find a group that looks interesting, then select it and click the Subscribe button

9 To find groups covering a particular subject, type a word that might appear in the name into the "Display..." box

10 Click the Subscribed tab to see a list of the groups you have selected

11 If you want to add more groups later on, select your news server from the Folders list. Click the Newsgroups button or select Tools>Newsgroups. You won't have to download the list again

Read the news

Reading newsgroup messages is slightly different from reading email. Instead of downloading all the messages, which might take some time, Outlook Express only fetches the headers (the sections that contains the subject line, sender's name and so on). You then download the ones that sound interesting.

1 Select your news server from the Folder list to display your subscribed newsgroups

Some groups are very busy and receive hundreds of new messages each day. To tell Outlook Express how many headers to fetch, select Tools> Options and click the Read tab. Enter a number in the "Get xx headers…" box.

2 Double-click one of the groups to download the message headers

3 Click a title to download and display the body of the message

News messages don't stay on the server forever; your service provider keeps clearing them out to make way for new ones. If a group is very busy, they may only be accessible for a day or two, so check popular groups regularly. You can search for old messages using Google's Group search at: http://groups.google.com/

4 Outlook Express displays ongoing conversations as "threads", with the responses immediately below the original message. Click the plus ⊞ and minus ⊟ icons to expand and contract the threads

Sorry, what?

Most people can't type well, so they use smileys and acronyms to speed things up. They can also clarify people's comments.

Smileys

Smileys are also known as emoticons. Don't use too many – some people think they're silly.

It's difficult to communicate your emotions in a brief text message to a stranger. This can lead to arguments, especially if you're prone to bluntness or sarcasm. Many people get round this problem by using "smileys" – little faces made out of keyboard characters – to convey their state of mind.

There arc dozens of different smileys. The three you're most likely to encounter are:

:-)	happy
;-)	winking or "only joking"
:-(	sad or disappointed

(Turn the book 90 degrees to the right to see the faces.)

Acronyms

Found an acronym you can't decipher? Use the Acronym Finder, at: http://www.acronymfinder.com/

Common phrases are often abbreviated to their initials, producing TLAs (Three-Letter Acronyms) and ETLAs (Extended TLAs). You'll also see phonetic abbreviations.

Common acronyms and abbreviations include:

AFAIK	As far as I know
B4	Before
BTW	By the way
F2F	Face to face
FYI	For your information
<g>	Grin
IMO	In my opinion
IMHO	In my humble opinion
IMNSHO	In my not so humble opinion
ISTM	It seems to me
ISTR	I seem to recall
IRL	In real life (meaning, off the Internet)
L8R	Later
ROFL	Rolling on floor laughing
RSN	Real soon now
RTFM	Read the "flipping" manual

Chat with your buddies

Instant messaging enables you to hold conversations over the Internet by typing messages back and forth. It's spontaneous, convenient and absurdly popular. This chapter explains how it works and gets you clacking on your keyboard.

Covers

Chapter Eleven

When you add someone to your Contacts list (Step 4), Windows Messenger lets them know. They have two options: they can allow you to contact them or block all your messages. Likewise, when someone adds you to their list, you can let them in or shut them out. This prevents total strangers from bothering you with irrelevant messages.

1 If you know the person and want to communicate with them, select "Allow this person…". You can add them to your own Contact list

To change the way your name is displayed or use a nickname instead, go to Tools>Options and click the Personal tab. Change the "My display name" setting.

2 If you've been added by someone you don't know (or don't like), choose "Block this person…"

3 If you change your mind about someone, go to Tools>Options. Click the Privacy tab and move the person from the Allow list to the Block list, or vice versa

Chat with your buddies

Instant messaging enables you to hold conversations over the Internet by typing messages back and forth. It's spontaneous, convenient and absurdly popular. This chapter explains how it works and gets you clacking on your keyboard.

Covers

Chapter Eleven

When you add someone to your Contacts list (Step 4), Windows Messenger lets them know. They have two options: they can allow you to contact them or block all your messages. Likewise, when someone adds you to their list, you can let them in or shut them out. This prevents total strangers from bothering you with irrelevant messages.

To change the way your name is displayed or use a nickname instead, go to Tools>Options and click the Personal tab. Change the "My display name" setting.

1   If you know the person and want to communicate with them, select "Allow this person…". You can add them to your own Contact list

2   If you've been added by someone you don't know (or don't like), choose "Block this person…"

3   If you change your mind about someone, go to Tools>Options. Click the Privacy tab and move the person from the Allow list to the Block list, or vice versa

Chat with your buddies

Instant messaging enables you to hold conversations over the Internet by typing messages back and forth. It's spontaneous, convenient and absurdly popular. This chapter explains how it works and gets you clacking on your keyboard.

Covers

Chapter Eleven

All the icons have keyboard shortcuts. To see the list, click the Emoticons button, then click the button with three dots ⬚. See page 162 for more about emoticons.

7 To convey humor or emotion, click the Emoticons button and choose an icon

If you have a microphone or video camera attached to your computer, you can also conduct audio or video conversations. Go to Help>Help Topics for more information.

When one of your buddies tries to contact you, the initial message pops up in the bottom right-hand corner of your screen.

1 Click the message to bring up the Conversation window

2 Carry on with the conversation by typing a reply into the bottom window

Chat with your buddies

Instant messaging enables you to hold conversations over the Internet by typing messages back and forth. It's spontaneous, convenient and absurdly popular. This chapter explains how it works and gets you clacking on your keyboard.

Covers

Chapter Eleven

...cont'd

All the icons have keyboard shortcuts. To see the list, click the Emoticons button, then click the button with three dots ▢ *. See page 162 for more about emoticons.*

7 To convey humor or emotion, click the Emoticons button and choose an icon

If you have a microphone or video camera attached to your computer, you can also conduct audio or video conversations. Go to Help>Help Topics for more information.

When one of your buddies tries to contact you, the initial message pops up in the bottom right-hand corner of your screen.

1 Click the message to bring up the Conversation window

2 Carry on with the conversation by typing a reply into the bottom window

Chat with your buddies

Instant messaging enables you to hold conversations over the Internet by typing messages back and forth. It's spontaneous, convenient and absurdly popular. This chapter explains how it works and gets you clacking on your keyboard.

Covers

Chapter Eleven

Instant messaging

When you communicate by email, message boards or newsgroups, the conversations can be frustratingly laconic. Messages sometimes go unanswered for hours or even days. If you find that annoying, you'll probably prefer instant messaging.

When you send an instant message, it pops up on the other person's screen immediately – assuming they are online and have activated their messaging program. It's the Internet equivalent of using your mobile phone to send a text (SMS) message.

If you have a broadband connection, you can also hook up a microphone or video camera so you can see and/or hear the other person. If you have to be away for Christmas, you might use messaging software to watch your family open their presents.

The big difference between instant messaging and the other services is that messaging enables people *who are online* to communicate with other people *who are online*. It's a real-time, interactive activity that needs a live connection.

The no-fuss, no-muss service

When you run an instant-messaging program, it notifies a central server that you're connected to the Internet and ready to receive messages. The server acts as a giant, global "in or out" board and keeps track of everyone's status.

You don't have to hunt through millions of names to find out whether your friends are online. Your messaging program automatically checks the status of your "contacts" or "buddies" and displays a list of people you can send messages to. This system makes instant messaging one of the simplest and friendliest Internet applications. The software tells you who is available and you double-click a person's name to send them a message. There are no addresses to remember (or forget).

Choose a messenger

When you're browsing the Web or sending email, it doesn't matter if you use a different program from your friends. There are rules governing the format of Web pages and email messages, so everyone can muddle along together.

Instant messaging isn't quite as organized. The software companies are all fighting for a share of the market and don't seem able to agree on anything. In general, if you have program A from company A is for Annoying, you can only communicate with other users of program A. You won't be able to send messages to people who use program B from company B is for Botheration. This is a frustrating state of affairs, but there isn't much sign of a solution. All you can do is ask your friends which program they use and go with the majority decision.

Choices, choices

Windows Messenger has been updated since Windows XP was released. Get the latest version from Microsoft's Download Center before you try to follow the instructions in this chapter.

If you have Windows XP, you already have an instant-messaging program called Windows Messenger. Friends who use older versions of Windows can install a similar program called MSN Messenger. It doesn't have Windows Messenger's more advanced features, but people with MSN Messenger can exchange messages with people who use Windows Messenger, and vice versa.

You can download the latest versions of Windows Messenger and MSN Messenger from Microsoft's Download Center, at: http://www.microsoft.com/download/

Other popular instant messaging programs include AOL Instant Messenger (AIM), ICQ ("I seek you") and Yahoo! Messenger. You can get more information about them from the following sites:

AOL, at: http://www.aol.com/
ICQ Inc, at: http://www.icq.com/
Yahoo!, at http://messenger.yahoo.com/

The rest of this chapter concentrates on Windows Messenger.

Get a .NET Passport

To find out more about Passports, visit the .NET Passport Web site. Find it at:
http://www.passport.com/

You'll need to sign up for a .NET Passport before you can use Windows Messenger.

.NET Passport is a centralized password service run by Microsoft. Once you have a Passport, you can use your email address and Passport password to log in to any site that uses this technology. The advantage of this system is that you only have one password to remember. However, if someone else discovers your password, they can pretend to be you on a number of sites.

You'll be asked to create a Passport when you try to use Microsoft services such as Hotmail (see page 145) and Windows Messenger.

1 Click the Start button and select All Programs>Windows Messenger. Select .Net Messaging Service and click OK

2 The Passport Wizard prompts you to create a Passport. Click Next to continue (and after each step)

3 When you're asked if you have an email address, click Yes. Click No when you are asked if you have already registered it

4 Your browser opens and takes you to the Passport Web site, where you can sign up for a Passport

...cont'd

If you have an email account with Hotmail or MSN.com, you already have a Passport. Click the Sign In button in Step 5 and enter your address and password.

5 Enter your email address

6 Think up a password and enter it twice

7 Complete the Registration check

8 Scroll down to the Terms of Use and Statement of Privacy and read them. Once you're happy to proceed, enter your email address and click I Agree

9 Your email address is registered as a Passport. Click Continue to return to the Passport Wizard

Associating the Passport with your Windows user account makes sense if you are the only person who uses your computer or if all the people who use it have their own accounts (that is, each person selects their own name from the Welcome screen when they turn on the computer). If several people use the computer from the same user account, don't associate the Passport.

10 The Wizard asks whether you want to associate the Passport with your user account. To do this, simply click Next, then Finish

11 You'll also get an email asking you to verify your address. Click the enclosed link

12 Follow the on-screen instructions to sign in and reconfirm your identity

Ready for a chat?

Windows Messenger may run automatically when you power up your computer. If it doesn't, you'll need to start it yourself.

1 Look for an icon showing a green, stylized person in the notification area at the right-hand end of the Windows taskbar. Double-click it to open the program window

2 If you can't find the icon, click the Start button and select All Programs, then Windows Messenger

3 If you've associated your Passport with your Windows user name (see previous page), you'll be signed in automatically. If not, you'll need to enter your email address and Passport password

4 You may be prompted to choose a screen name

5 Windows Messenger contacts the central server and informs it that you're online and ready to receive messages

Find your buddies

The next thing to do is to add your friends to your Contacts list, so you can send messages to them easily. You'll need to know their email addresses.

If your friend has more than one email address, you'll need to find out which one they use for their .NET Passport.

1 Click the "Add a Contact" link in the "I want to…" list at the bottom

2 Select "By email address or sign-in name". Click Next

3 Enter your friend's email address

4 Windows Messenger checks with the central server and tries to locate your friend. If it succeeds, their name is added to your Contact list

5 If your friend isn't using Windows Messenger, you can't add them to your list. You're invited to send them an email that explains how to download and install the software

When you add someone to your Contacts list (Step 4), Windows Messenger lets them know. They have two options: they can allow you to contact them or block all your messages. Likewise, when someone adds you to their list, you can let them in or shut them out. This prevents total strangers from bothering you with irrelevant messages.

1   If you know the person and want to communicate with them, select "Allow this person…". You can add them to your own Contact list

To change the way your name is displayed or use a nickname instead, go to Tools>Options and click the Personal tab. Change the "My display name" setting.

2   If you've been added by someone you don't know (or don't like), choose "Block this person…"

3   If you change your mind about someone, go to Tools>Options. Click the Privacy tab and move the person from the Allow list to the Block list, or vice versa

Start a conversation

Windows Messenger shows you which of your contacts are online. Glance at the list to find out who's available for a chat.

1 To contact one of your buddies, double-click their name

2 Type a message into the bottom window

3 Click Send

4 The message pops up on the other person's screen. If they feel like chatting, you'll get a reply in a few seconds

5 The reply appears in the top window

6 To carry on chatting, type another comment into the bottom window and click Send again

If you can't type very quickly, use abbreviations to speed things up. Try "u" for "you", "cu" for "see you" and "l8r" for "later".

All the icons have keyboard shortcuts. To see the list, click the Emoticons button, then click the button with three dots ⌷. *See page 162 for more about emoticons.*

7 To convey humor or emotion, click the Emoticons button and choose an icon

If you have a microphone or video camera attached to your computer, you can also conduct audio or video conversations. Go to Help>Help Topics for more information.

When one of your buddies tries to contact you, the initial message pops up in the bottom right-hand corner of your screen.

1 Click the message to bring up the Conversation window

2 Carry on with the conversation by typing a reply into the bottom window

Build a Web site

You came, you saw, you clicked… and now it's time to stop touring and start designing your own pages. A Web site can serve all sorts of useful purposes, from promoting your business to sharing the photographs from your wedding, or it can simply be something you create for fun. This chapter explains what's involved and helps you lay the foundations.

Covers

Chapter Twelve

A site of your own

There'll come a day when you want to create Web pages. You'll be wandering around the Web, clicking from page to page, and suddenly you'll want a site of your own – a virtual home that promotes your business, showcases your interests and/or reflects your personality.

There are lots of reasons to create a Web site:

- **To advertise your services.** If you go online for business reasons, creating a Web site is probably near the top of your to-do list. It's a great (and inexpensive) way to explain what you offer and stay in touch with your customers.

- **To promote yourself.** If you're looking for a job, an online resume not only provides information about your education and experience, but also demonstrates that you're at home in the high-tech world of the Internet. Online portfolios are also useful for people who work on a freelance basis, such as writers, photographers, programmers and consultants.

- **To share your interests.** If you have a passion for a particular subject, creating a Web site lets you make use of the material you've accumulated. You can pass on information to other enthusiasts and get more out of your hobby. You might not want to go scuba diving in the middle of the winter, for example, but you can still work on your diving Web pages.

- **Keep your friends and family up to date.** A personal Web site is the best way to share stories and photographs from family events and holidays. You only have to tell each story once and you can add as many pictures as you want.

- **It's fun.** Creating a Web site is like decorating your home, except you don't have to wash the brushes or wait for the paint to dry. You get to choose the subject, the colors, the fonts and the design. It's a chance to exercise your creativity and produce something that's uniquely yours.

This chapter won't teach you everything about creating a Web site, but it'll get you started. If you want to learn more, look out for "Web Page Design in easy steps" and other titles in this series.

Learn the lingo

Web pages are created using HyperText Mark-up Language, otherwise known as HTML. You can produce HTML files with a word processor, but most people prefer to use a dedicated HTML editor – a program designed specifically for creating Web pages.

Tag it and bag it

The simplest approach to HTML is to start with a file containing the text for your page. You then "mark up" the text by inserting tags – commands that tell Web browsers how to format individual words, phrases and paragraphs.

Most tags come in pairs: an "on" tag that goes before the text you want to format and an "off" tag that goes afterwards. Both of the tags are surrounded by angled brackets. For example:

This is my <b>very first</b> Web page.

The <b> tag turns on bold formatting and the </b> tag turns it off again, giving:

This is my **very first** Web page.

There are tags that control different types of formatting, tags that tell browsers to insert an image file or create a link, and tags that take care of housekeeping tasks, such as giving the page a name. HTML is just a toolbox of instructions that enable you to turn a slab of text into a formatted Web page.

All your own <yawn> work

In the early days of the Web, people created their pages by hand. They started with a text file and added tags in all the right places, painstakingly inserting angled brackets until the page was complete.

The good thing about creating pages by hand is that you become intimately familiar with all the tags. The bad thing is that it's incredibly tedious. It's also easy to make mistakes. If you add a <b> tag and then forget to add the corresponding </b>, the bold formatting continues to the end of the page. Every page has to be checked in a Web browser, and edited, and checked again.

Today most people use visual HTML editors that display the actual formatting, rather than the tags. Instead of entering <b> and </b>, you highlight the text you want to format, then click the

Bold button or select Bold from the Format menu. The program inserts the corresponding tags.

You design a page like this...   ...and your editor adds the tags

With a visual editor, designing a Web page is like formatting any other document. You can create an entire site without knowing anything about HTML. However, if you're serious about Web design, it helps to understand the basics. Some of the things you can do in a word processor don't work in HTML, and vice versa.

Choosing an HTML editor

You can use almost anything to design Web pages: a basic text editor such as Notepad, a word processor, a desktop-publishing program or even a graphics program. However, it's best to use a tool that was designed for the job. A dedicated HTML editor enables you to create attractive Web pages, quickly and efficiently.

Big-name HTML editors include Adobe's GoLive, Macromedia's Dreamweaver and Microsoft's FrontPage. However, these are professional programs with correspondingly impressive price tags. More affordable alternatives includes Namo's WebEditor, the program used for the step-by-step guides in this chapter.

You can get more information about these programs from the following Web sites:

Adobe, at: http://www.adobe.com/
Macromedia, at: http://www.macromedia.com/
Microsoft, at: http://www.microsoft.com/
SJ Namo Interactive, at: http://www.namo.com/

Plan your site

The key to successful Web design is to plan your site on paper before you start creating the pages. The structure of your site affects the construction of the links, so if you get it wrong, you'll have to go through your pages and change all the links – which is annoying, to put it mildly.

Start with a sketch

Find a piece of paper and draw a doodle that shows all the pages of your Web site and the most important links between them. For example, here's a plan for a personal Web site:

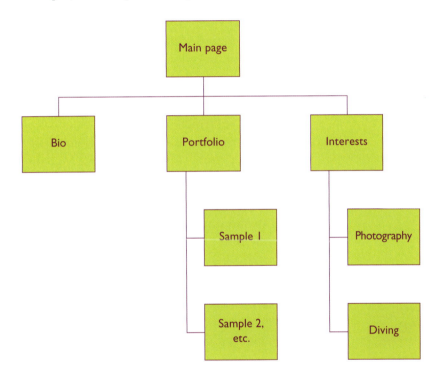

Think about pages you may want to add later. Where will they go? Ensure your plan is flexible enough to let the site evolve and grow.

Files and folders

For a small site, you can keep all your files in a single folder. For larger sites, it's a good idea to create a folder for the site, then add a subfolder for each section. Otherwise you'll end up with a big, unmanageable heap of files.

Be very careful when you name your files. Since people use all kinds of computers to access the Internet, it's a good idea to choose names that will work on any system. That means:

• Up to eight lowercase letters, followed by a dot (period), followed by a three-character extension.

• No punctuation, other than periods (.) and underlines (_), and no funny characters.

• The extension should be .htm for a Web page and .gif or .jpg for an image (see below).

Give your documents meaningful names such as bio.htm and portfol.htm. If you call them page01.htm, page02.htm and so on, you'll find it hard to tell them apart when you want to edit them. Record the names on your sketch.

File formats

Web pages are saved as plain (unformatted) text documents, but with a .htm extension. Your HTML editor will take care of that (one of the advantages of using a proper HTML editor is that it automatically saves files in the correct format).

Pictures must be saved in either the GIF format (.gif extension) or the JPEG format (.jpg extension). The GIF format is usually the right choice for artwork such as logos, buttons, diagrams, maps and cartoons. The JPEG format is used for photographs.

Learn more about Paint Shop Pro from Jasc's Web site, at: http:// www.jasc.com/

Your images may already be in the correct format. For example, if you are using photographs from a digital camera, they are probably .jpg files already. If you are creating original graphics, or you have pictures in other formats, you'll need to use an image-editing program such as Paint Shop Pro to save them as GIFs or JPEGs.

An image editor also comes in handy if your images aren't the right size for your Web site. Images on Web sites must be kept small to minimize the file size and reduce the download time. You may need to scale down existing images before you use them on your Web pages.

Work with words

The text forms the backbone of your Web page. You can type it directly into a new page or cut and paste the text from an existing document, such as an essay or report.

1 Run your HTML editor and create a new Web page. Save it

2 Enter your text

Only use fonts that other Internet users will have: Arial, Comic Sans, Georgia, Impact, Times New Roman, Trebuchet and Verdana.

3 Use the text-formatting tools to choose a font and change the size, color and style

The title appears at the top of the Web browser window, in the blue title bar. Keep it short. When someone makes a Favorite for this Web page, the title will end up in their Favorites menu.

4 To give the page a title, go to File>Document Properties and click the General tab. Enter the title

5 Save the Web page

Add some pictures

Before you add an image to your Web page, ask yourself the following questions:

- **Is the image the right size?** Open it in an image-editing program and check the dimensions, in pixels. You may need to reduce the size to fit it on to your page.

- **Has the image been saved in a Web-friendly format?** It must be a .gif or .jpg file.

- **Is the image in the correct folder?** You can put it in the same folder as the Web page document or create a special subfolder for image files. Be consistent, though.

1 Open a Web page in your HTML editor and position the cursor where you want the image to appear. It's a good idea to put it in a separate paragraph

2 Go to Insert>Image> Image... or click the Insert Image button

3 Click the Browse button and find the image file. Click Open and then OK to add it to the Web page

4 The image appears on your page

To center an image, select the paragraph in which it appears. Use the text-formatting tools to center the entire paragraph.

5 Insert more images in the same paragraph to produce a horizontal row of pictures

6 Add images in separate paragraphs to produce a vertical column

7 If you arrange the images vertically, you can type short captions alongside them. To adjust the placement of the caption, right-click on the image and select Image Properties. Set "Alignment" to "Top", "Middle" or "Bottom". For a long caption, select "Left"

Create hyperlinks

Creating a link is simple: you select the text (or image) you want to link from, then open a dialog box and enter the address of the page you want to link to. There's just one catch: you must get your files and folders in order before you start creating links.

Suppose you have two Web pages stored in the same folder on your hard disk. When you create a link from the first page to the second, you add an instruction that tells your Web browser to go back to the folder where it found the first page and look for the second one. The link doesn't specify the name or location of the folder. It just says, "Same again, Sam, but grab page2.htm". In Web-design terms, it's a "relative reference".

The important thing about this system is that you can move both pages to a different folder – for example, a folder on your service provider's Web server – without breaking the link. As long as the pages are together, your Web browser can find the second one.

If you find this system confusing, keep all your Web pages in a single folder.

The pages don't have to be in the same folder to make this work. For example, you could put the second page in a subfolder. The link would then tell your Web browser to go back to the original folder, then down into subfolder, then find the second page. As long as you use the same folders on the Web server, and arrange them in the same way, the links will work.

1 To link two of your own pages together, select the text you want to link from

2 Select Insert>Hyperlink or click the Insert Hyperlink button

3 Click the Browse button and select the page you want to link to. Click Open and then OK

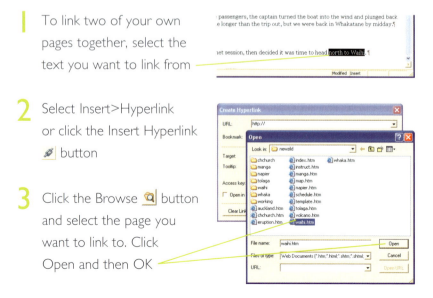

4 The text becomes a link

You may also want to link to other people's Web pages, or turn some of your images into links. The procedures are similar.

1 To link to a page on someone else's Web site, you must fill in the entire address, including the http://

2 To link from an image, for example to create a clickable button, start by inserting the image (see page 180). Click on the image to select it, then follow Steps 2 and 3 on the opposite page

Tidy up with tables

Tables are used to organize information into rows and columns. They're useful for price lists, schedules, competition results and so on. Less obviously, they can be used to control the layout of your Web page. For example, you might use a table to divide the page into two columns, one for pictures and one for text.

I To create a table, place the cursor where you want it to appear. Go to Table>New Table

You can also set the width of the table, in pixels or as a percentage of the browser window. Cell Spacing sets the space between the cells; Cell Padding sets the space between the cell border and the contents of the cell. If you set Border Thickness to 0, the borders disappear.

2 Specify the number of rows and columns you require

3 An empty table is inserted. The cells expand and contract as you fill in your information

Find space for your site

Your Web pages need to be stored or "hosted" on a computer that's permanently connected to the Internet, so everyone can access them. There are three options:

- Your Internet service provider may give you some space on its Web server as part of your Internet account. This is often the best option, because there's no additional cost involved. Check with your service provider to find out how much space you have and how you access it. Check the terms and conditions, too – sometimes you're only allowed to use the space for a personal, noncommercial Web site.

- If you didn't get any Web space with your account, you can sign up with one of the services that provide free hosting. Like Web-based mail services, companies that offer free hosting are supported by advertising. When people visit your site, they'll also see adverts that have been added by the hosting company. Popular services include Tripod (at http://www.tripod.lycos.com/) and Yahoo! GeoCities (at http://geocities.yahoo.com/).

- If you're setting up a Web site for your business, you won't want to display someone else's ads. A more professional option is to rent space from a company that specializes in hosting Web sites. In return for a monthly or annual fee, you'll get plenty of space for your site. You may also get extra services such as technical support, information about your visitors and the option to add interactive features such as password protection or message boards. Flick through a couple of Internet magazines to find out what's available.

A name to be proud of

If your Web space is provided by your service provider, or by one of the free Web-hosting services, you'll end up with a complicated Web address such as:

> http://www.someservice.com/~joe/

See page 46-47 for more about domain names.

By the time you've spelled it out a dozen times for your family, your friends and your colleagues at work, you'll be wishing it was shorter and easier to remember. The solution is to register your own domain name, such as:

> joeordinary.com

You can then change your Web address to:

> http://www.joeordinary.com/

You can also have a new email address, such as:

> mail@joeordinary.com

Just as there are companies that concentrate on hosting Web sites, there are companies that specialize in registering domain names (and many that do both). Search for "domain name registration" or look through adverts in Internet magazines to find a company that can help.

Domain names must be unique, so only one person can have joeordinary.com

However, there can also be:

* *joeordinary.org*
* *joeordinary.name*
* *joeordinary.co.uk*

and so on.

Some companies offer a budget package that includes the name of your choice (assuming it is still available) plus Web and email forwarding. With Web forwarding, anyone who enters your new address is automatically taken to your existing Web site. You don't have to move the site or change it in any way. Likewise, if someone sends email to your new address, it is sent on to your existing mail box. One advantage of this system is that it doesn't matter if you change Internet service providers. You just update the forwarding details so people (and messages) get shunted to your new location.

If you rent Web space from a hosting company, you'll probably get a domain name thrown in. It'll be set up to point to your Web site, so you don't have to worry about forwarding.

Index

Q

R

S

T

Worldwide Web Guide

Alphabetical list of sites

News

Whether you're looking for breaking news or archived stories, the Web is the best place to start. Most of the major broadcasters and publishers have Web sites that are updated throughout the day. Search functions and electronic cross-references make it easy to find stories of interest and follow them back to their roots.

Resources

Google News

http://news.google.com/

Google News pulls together stories from over 4,000 news sources and compiles them into a single page. Follow the links for more information or use the search function to hunt down particular items.

Yahoo! News

http://news.yahoo.com/

Yahoo! gives you a well-organized overview of the top stories, with dedicated areas for major events and issues. Special features include slideshows that bring together the best photographs, message boards and a Most Popular section that lists the stories other Internet users are reading. You can search for news stories, photographs and audio or video.

Guardian Unlimited World News Guide

http://www.guardian.co.uk/worldnewsguide/

Guardian Unlimited's attractively presented News Guide links you to news sources and government Web sites from around the world, by region or country. The directory is selective – you get the best sites, not a comprehensive list – making it a good place to start your research.

Abyz News Links

http://www.abyznewslinks.com/

Abyz News Links is functional rather than attractive. It provides a comprehensive database of online newspapers, broadcasters and other news sources, sorted by country. Details include the type of media, the focus (general, business, sport and so on) and the language used. The listings are searchable.

World-newspapers.com

http://www.world-newspapers.com/

This site is less specialized than it sounds. It deals in magazines as well as newspapers and has links to the main sources of news in various subject areas, including world, business, Internet and sport. It also lists sites that offer photographs, personalized news services, alternative news and criticism.

Onlinenewspapers.com

http://www.onlinenewspapers.com/

This site presents a well-organized database of online newspapers, sorted by country. There's no information about the papers, apart from an occasional note about the language, but you can find what you want very quickly.

HeadlineSpot.com

http://www.headlinespot.com/

HeadlineSpot is a US-oriented site that lists resources by type and subject. It's especially useful for specialized areas such as columnists, polls, industry news and obituaries.

NewsNow

http://www.newsnow.co.uk/

NewsNow aggregates headlines from a range of (primarily British) online sources, presenting a single-page view of the day's top stories. You can also opt to focus on topical issues or areas, from Bin Laden and Iraq to soap operas and Harry Potter.

Findory

http://www.findory.com/

Interesting site that recompiles its front page every time you click a link, adjusting its content to match your reading habits. It catalogues Weblogs (personal journals) as well as traditional news sources.

BBC News by email

http://www.bbc.co.uk/dailyemail/

If you don't have time for the Web, get the BBC to email you a daily bulletin covering the subjects of your choice. Options include UK and world news, politics, business, health and sport.

Broadcast news

CNN

http://www.cnn.com/

CNN offers two editions – US and International – and has sections for everything from US and world news to sport, technology, politics, health, travel and entertainment. CNN's long-standing interest in the US space program makes it particularly strong in that area.

Voice of America

http://www.voanews.com/

The US government's broadcasting service transmits in 44 languages. Read the latest stories or tune in to audio and video Webcasts. Special features include a pronunciation guide that helps you say the names of newsworthy people and places.

MSNBC

http://www.msnbc.com/news/

The MSNBC Web site offers an upbeat take on the news with multimedia and interactive features.

BBC News

http://news.bbc.co.uk/

The BBC has an excellent news site with everything you could want: UK, international and foreign-language editions, streaming audio and video, a text-only version for slow connections, in-depth features and a wealth of breaking news, all served up without adverts or other distractions.

BBC World Service

http://www.bbc.co.uk/worldservice/

The World Service site comes in 43 languages. It offers short audio bulletins on demand plus the opportunity to tune in to a 24-hour news channel or the regular World Service broadcasts.

ITN

http://www.itn.co.uk/

ITN provides news for the UK's commercial television channels – ITV, Channel 4 and Channel 5 – and virtually all the commercial radio stations. Follow the links for news bulletins from your favorite broadcaster.

Sky News

http://www.sky.com/skynews/

British broadcaster Sky News gives you more pictures than most. There are lots of photo galleries and it has Webcams that enable you to spy on popular locations in London and Edinburgh.

CBC

http://www.cbc.ca/

The Canadian Broadcasting Corporation delivers news to wireless devices such as mobile phones and PDAs, sends headlines to your email inbox and broadcasts audio bulletins over the Internet.

ABC News Online

http://www.abc.net.au/news/

The news section of ABC's site has both Australian and international news, with special sections for rural and indigenous news. Other features include audio, video, forums and news by email.

Channelnewsasia.com

http://www.channelnewsasia.com/

Channel NewsAsia's Web site has Singapore, Asia-Pacific and world news. Special features include news formatted for handheld computers.

Radio New Zealand

http://www.radionz.co.nz/

Radio New Zealand broadcasts news bulletins and selected programs over the Internet, in Windows Media format. You can also click through to the Radio NZ International site for a selection of stories from the Pacific.

Newswires

Reuters

http://www.reuters.com/

The famous news agency offers both regular and business news on a jam-packed Web site. Beyond the usual sections, there's an Oddly Enough area featuring stories such as "Record Warm Winter Stirs Sleepy Estonian Bears". The Reuters site also has extensive photo galleries dedicated to news, entertainment, sports and fashion.

Associated Press

http://www.ap.org/

The Associated Press Web site doesn't provide news directly; instead, it links you to member sites in the US and elsewhere. Clicking a link takes you to a randomly chosen site carrying the story you selected. For a fee, you can search the AP Archive.

Ananova

http://www.ananova.com/

Ananova's unique selling point is a green-haired, computer-generated virtual newsreader who delivers bulletins in a synthetic voice. You can opt for regular, light, sporty or quirky news, or simply read the stories yourself. Ananova also sends news to mobile phones on the UK's Orange network.

News24

http://www.news24.com/

News24 is a South African service providing local, African and international news. Special reports provide in-depth coverage of major events such as elections and important issues such as HIV/AIDS.

Newspapers and magazines

The New York Times

http://www.nytimes.com/

The online edition of *The New York Times* is so newspaper-like in both layout and content that you wonder why there's no ink on your hands when you finish reading. It's a literate, in-depth antidote to the infobite news that dominates the Internet.

Washington Post

http://www.washingtonpost.com/

The Washington Post's Web site has a special section for politics, where you'll find the latest news from the White House, the Senate and Congress. You may even find coverage of Watergate, a mere three decades after the paper first broke the story.

Chicago Tribune

http://www.chicagotribune.com/

Daily news from Chicago. The *Tribune* has a strong sports section, even though the local teams aren't currently enjoying the glory the Chicago Bulls experienced in the 1990s.

USA Today

http://www.usatoday.com/

A more concise take on the news from the national newspaper. The online edition includes fun features such as an interactive crossword.

Christian Science Monitor

http://www.csmonitor.com/

For a different perspective, try the online edition of *Christian Science Monitor*, an international, Pulitzer prize-winning daily newspaper published by the First Church of Christ, Scientist. Its mission is "to injure no man, but to bless all mankind."

Time

http://www.time.com/time/

News, in-depth features, photo essays and opinion columns from the weekly magazine. You can also go back in *TIME* and look at the covers and cover stories from fifty-odd years ago.

Telegraph.co.uk

http://www.telegraph.co.uk/

The UK's leading online newspaper has everything, including news, business news, sport, motoring, shopping, gardening, weather, opinions, horoscopes, crosswords (requires an annual subscription), letters, obituaries and cartoons. Best of all, it has an enormous, searchable archive going all the way back to April 1996 – and there's no charge for retrieving stories.

Times Online

http://www.timesonline.co.uk/

The online edition of *The Times* presents itself in a more subdued, newspaper-like fashion. There's even an option to view virtual versions of the papers from the last seven days, so you can see which stories were published together. It also has a series of online specials, but it lacks the free archive that makes *The Telegraph's* site so useful.

Guardian Unlimited

http://www.guardian.co.uk/

Guardian Unlimited is more sectionized than most newspaper sites, enabling you to concentrate entirely on news, sport, politics or whatever else takes your fancy. Spin-off sections for film and football feel even more divorced from the main site. It's a more Internetty, less newspapery approach.

The Sun Newspaper Online

http://www.thesun.co.uk/

The UK's biggest-selling newspaper has a cheerful site that reflects its tabloid nature with punchy headlines, celebrity gossip and a huge gallery of Page 3 photographs.

News.com.au

http://news.com.au/

News.com.au brings together stories from the News Limited network, which comprises over 100 Australian newspapers. Members include *The Australian*, *The Daily Telegraph*, the *Herald Sun*, *The Courier-Mail*, *The Advertiser*, *The Mercury* and *The Sunday Times*. Special features include audio reports and news by email.

Sydney Morning Herald

http://www.smh.com.au/

The Sydney Morning Herald's site covers the usual newspaper ground, with a couple of interesting additions. You can download a PDF file of the paper's front page, for the authentic newspaper experience, and there's a Webdiary that mixes commentary from one of the journalists with feedback from her readers.

The New Zealand Herald

http://www.nzherald.co.nz/

Across the Tasman, *The New Zealand Herald* has a simple site with New Zealand and world news, plus business, technology, sports, entertainment and travel sections. PDA users can subscribe to a compact version and download it to their Palm or Pocket PC palmtop computer.

Stuff

http://www.stuff.co.nz/

Stuff brings together stories from New Zealand newspapers such as *The Waikato Times*, *The Dominion Post*, *The Press* and *The Southland Times*. Rural, regional, national and world news stories all have their place.

globeandmail.com

http://www.theglobeandmail.com/

The Web site of Canada's *The Globe and Mail* newspaper has free breaking news and special features, plus a subscription-based Insider Edition.

Mail&Guardian Online

http://www.mg.co.za/

South Africa's Mail&Guardian Online has been publishing news on the Internet since 1994. In addition to South African and African news, it has specialist features such as a Notes and Queries section and an HIV/AIDS barometer.

The Straits Times Interactive

http://straitstimes.asia1.com.sg/

Strait Times Interactive has a selection of stories from the current edition of *The Straits Times*, Singapore's most popular broadsheet. There's a limited free archive with articles from the three previous days. For anything older, you have to pay.

Wall Street Journal

http://online.wsj.com/

The online edition of *The Wall Street Journal* comes in three flavors, for the US, Europe and Asia. Brief stories on the front page lead you to more detailed articles in the interior, making it an easy site to browse – if you're prepared to pay for an annual subscription. Free content hides near the bottom of the front page and includes annual reports.

Bloomberg.com

http://www.bloomberg.com/

Bloomberg's Web site has financial news, market reports, stock prices and a range of financial tools.

Forbes.com

http://www.forbes.com/

Cast an envious eye over the names on the various lists – richest people, top celebrities and so on – then read the business, technology and market news to work out how to join them. Once you've acquired your millions, the Lifestyle section will help you spend them.

Business Week Online

http://www.businessweek.com/

Why wait a week when this US Web site brings you a daily dose of business news? Separate sections cover investing, global business, technology, small business and business education.

Financial Times

http://news.ft.com/

Although the pages are white rather than pink, the online edition of Britain's best-known business paper is as authoritative as the printed one. Some features require a paid subscription.

Economist.com

http://www.economist.com/

If you're concerned about global economics rather than your personal fortune, try the online edition of *The Economist.* Useful features include country data files with facts, figures and articles about the economic and political outlook.

Business 2.0

http://www.business2.com/

Find out what's happening in the new economy with news, features and commentary from *Business 2.0* magazine. If you don't find what you're looking for here, there's also a Web Guide that catalogs the best business sites.

SI.com

http://sportsillustrated.cnn.com/

Featuring material from CNN and *Sports Illustrated,* SI.com is dominated by baseball, basketball, football and ice hockey. It does a reasonable job of world sport as well, but don't expect obsessive coverage of sports such as cricket, soccer and rugby.

ESPN

http://espn.go.com/

ESPN offers more variety, with extensive coverage of soccer (as in football), golf and outdoor sports such as fishing and hunting. Many other sports are covered in the Olympic Sports section. For extreme sports such as skateboarding, snowboarding and bike stunt, visit EXPN.com (http://expn.go.com/).

BBC Sport

http://news.bbc.co.uk/sport/

BBC Sport covers football, cricket, rugby, tennis, golf, motorsport, boxing, athletics and other sports, with typical BBC thoroughness. You can watch, listen, vote, comment, play games or test your knowledge in the Question of Sport section.

Sporting Life

http://www.sportinglife.com/

UK sports paper *Sporting Life* concentrates on all the sports that Britons might take part in (or, more probably, watch and place bets on): football, horse racing, cricket, rugby, Formula 1, golf and so on.

Eurosport

http://www.eurosport.com/

Cable/satellite channel Eurosport offers news and results in several languages. Like the channel itself, the Web site doesn't shy away from less popular sports such as cycling, sailing, skiing and swimming. You can tune in to its broadcasts over the Internet, although you may hear more than you see.

SLAM! Sports

http://slam.canoe.ca/

Billing itself as "Canada's Home Page for Sports", this site has hockey (as in ice hockey) at the top of its list of sports, followed by football, followed by all the usual suspects in alphabetical order.

Sportal.com.au

http://sportal.com.au/

This Aussie sports portal covers a wide range of sports including cricket, rugby, Aussie Rules football, tennis, cycling and horse racing. It also has photo galleries, video, polls and games.

Weather

The Weather Channel

http://www.weather.com/

The Weather Channel's Web site has lots of US-oriented content. It also provides forecasts for the entire globe – just enter the name of a city for current conditions and predictions for the next ten days. You can choose between metric and imperial measurements and check the temperature and rainfall against the monthly averages.

BBC Weather

http://www.bbc.co.uk/weather/

The BBC's Weather site has five-day forecasts for the UK and the world, plus a wealth of weather-related information. Curious about climate change? Want to know the difference between ground frost and air frost? Wondering how the weather will affect upcoming sporting events? The BBC has all the answers.

CNN Weather

http://www.cnn.com/WEATHER/

Still haven't found acceptable weather? CNN gives you forecasts, temperatures and maps, by continent or city. Try animating the satellite maps to see cloud movements over the last six hours.

UK Met Office

http://www.metoffice.com/

The Met Office doesn't just forecast UK and world weather, it also provides a summary of the UK weather over the last month – just in case you weren't paying attention. It has an excellent range of satellite images and a set of Webcams that show you exactly what's happening around the UK.

PA WeatherCentre

http://www.paweathercentre.com/

The Press Association's WeatherCentre is notable for its groovy animated maps showing conditions around the UK. It also has a roundup of weather-related news stories.

Australian Bureau of Meteorology

http://www.bom.gov.au/

The Bureau of Meteorology provides a bunch of forecasts, charts, and radar and satellite images. There's also a special section for marine weather, with forecasts for coastal waters and high seas, current observations and links to tide tables. You'll need to be weather-savvy to interpret all the details.

NZ MetService

http://www.metservice.co.nz/

The MetService has a chatty site that provides easy access to regular, mountain and marine forecasts. The Learning Centre has climate data and articles on New Zealand weather. Look in the FAQ & Help area to find out how to read weather maps.

The Weather Network

http://www.theweathernetwork.com/

The Weather Network provides all sorts of forecasts for Canadians, including farming, golfing, ski-ing, marine and highway reports. In winter there's even a flu report with a map showing how many people are getting sick in each province.

National Environment Agency

http://app.nea.gov.sg/

Singapore's National Environment Agency (NEA) provides weather reports and haze readings. Forecasts are succinct, reflecting the predictability of Singapore's weather – try the station reports for more details. A frequently updated map of rain locations helps you work out whether you're experiencing an isolated shower or the opening salvo in a major storm.

South African Weather Service

http://www.weathersa.co.za/

The South African Weather Service provides general and specialized forecasts, radar and satellite images and real-time data. The Drought Monitoring Desk has overviews of the last six months and 30 days, plus seasonal forecasts and information about weather modification.

Information

The Internet isn't just entertaining, it's also incredibly useful. You can find everything from the capital of Kazakstan to the phone number of your next-door neighbor – if you know where to look. This section of the Worldwide Web Guide catalogs all the reference sites that come in handy when you're looking for facts and figures.

Resources

Bartleby.com

http://www.bartleby.com/

Bartleby.com has an extensive collection of reference books, including *The Columbia Encyclopedia*, *The American Heritage Dictionary*, *Roget's Thesaurus*, *The Oxford Shakespeare*, *The King James Bible* and *Gray's Anatomy*. While you don't always get the most recent edition, access is free and you can search individual titles, works of a particular type (such as Dictionaries) or the whole collection.

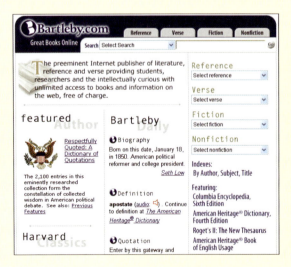

Refdesk

http://www.refdesk.com/

Refdesk is a gigantic catalog of reference Web sites. It's well organized, pointing you to the most useful resources first and then allowing you to dig deeper if necessary.

iTools

http://www.itools.com/

iTools provides easy access to a range of reference sites. Search the Web, look up words, find facts, convert currencies and look at maps.

Yahoo! Reference

http://education.yahoo.com/reference/

Yahoo!'s Reference page provides access to a selection of books and tools, including The Columbia Electronic Encyclopedia.

MSN Learning & Research

http://encarta.msn.com/

MSN's Learning and Research section provides access to material from Microsoft's Encarta Encyclopedia, World English Dictionary and Dynamic Atlas. Some articles are only available to MSN subscribers.

Encyclopedias

Encyclopaedia Britannica

http://www.britannica.com/

The 32-volume *Encyclopaedia Britannica*, online and searchable. The catch is that while some material can be browsed freely, you have to pay an annual subscription for full access. A free trial enables you to find out whether it's worth it.

Encyclopedia.com

http://www.encyclopedia.com/

Free access to 57,000 articles from *The Columbia Encyclopedia, Sixth Edition*. If you're a paid-up member of Highbeam Research, you can get further details using the links at the end of each article.

Dictionaries

OneLook Dictionaries

http://www.onelook.com/

Search for your word in over 800 online dictionaries using OneLook's simple interface. It's a useful tool that gives you quick access to multiple definitions. You can also find translations for foreign words.

Dictionary.com

http://dictionary.reference.com/

Dictionary.com also searches for your word in multiple dictionaries, although the selection is more limited. On the plus side, you can see the entries side by side and compare them. It also has a thesaurus, a translator and a Word of the Day feature.

Merriam-Webster OnLine

http://www.m-w.com/

Free access to the *Merriam-Webster Collegiate Dictionary* and *Collegiate Thesaurus*, plus subscription-based access to other dictionaries. Probably the Web's most popular dictionary, mostly because it has been available online for several years. Sound clips help you pronounce the words.

WordCentral.com

http://www.wordcentral.com/

WordCentral.com is aimed at younger Internet users. It enables you to search Merriam-Webster's *Student Dictionary* and has fun features such as a buzzword of the day, a verse composer and a Build Your Own Dictionary section for made-up words.

AskOxford

http://www.askoxford.com/

Wordy offerings from Oxford Publishing, including a word of the day, word games, articles about words and an Ask the Experts section. You can also get very concise definitions from the *Compact Oxford English Dictionary*.

Oxford English Dictionary

http://www.oed.com/

The famous and prestigious *Oxford English Dictionary*, available online – but only if you pay for an annual subscription. Otherwise you get a sample word each day. You never know, it might be the one you were looking for.

Cambridge Dictionaries Online

http://dictionary.cambridge.org/

Cambridge provides online access to seven dictionaries, including the *Cambridge Dictionary of American English, Cambridge Advanced*

Learner's Dictionary and *Cambridge Dictionary of Idioms*. A well-designed interface enables you to switch dictionaries without changing words. There's also a Word of the Day and a Top 20 section that reveals the most searched-for words.

Roget's Thesauri

http://www.bartleby.com/thesauri/

A number of Web sites provide access to *Roget's Thesaurus*, but Bartleby.com has the nicest interface. It provides synonyms from two versions, one from 1922 and the other from 1995.

Acronym Finder

http://www.acronymfinder.com/

Decipher annoying acronyms and abbreviations with the Acronym Finder, which has a database of over 380,000 confusing combinations of characters.

Jargon File

http://jargon.watson-net.com/

Also known, in its printed form, as *The New Hacker's Dictionary*, the Jargon File is something of an Internet institution. It lists and defines the jargon used by computer enthusiasts – "hackers" in the old sense, meaning people "who enjoy exploring the details of programmable systems and how to stretch their capabilities, as opposed to most users, who prefer to learn only the minimum necessary."

WordSpy

http://www.wordspy.com/

An entertaining site dedicated to new words and phrases. Each term gets a definition, an example of its use and a bit of background tracing its origin. Fascinating reading, even if you have little practical use for phrases such as "parachute children" and "corridor cruising".

Symbols.com

http://www.symbols.com/

A dictionary without words. Looking up symbols is slightly tricky, there being no such thing as alphabetical order when you're dealing with nonalphabetic characters, but Symbol.com gets round this with a question-and-answer page that helps you describe your graphic. If you know the meaning of your symbol, you can also work backwards from the list of definitions.

Grammar and style

Garbl's Writing Center

http://garbl.home.comcast.net/

Useful roundup of writing resources with links to many Web sites covering punctuation, spelling, grammar, style and other troublesome subjects. You can also get advice on the writing process.

Times Style Guide

http://www.timesonline.co.uk/

Find the link for the Style Guide at the bottom of the front page of Times Online and write like a top-notch journalist. It answers tricky questions such as whether to hyphenate "deckchair" (no) and how to spell "whiz-kid" (one "z").

Internet Grammar of English

http://www.ucl.ac.uk/internet-grammar/

Comprehensive guide to English grammar from University College London. It's aimed at students but is available to everyone.

Guide to Grammar and Style

http://andromeda.rutgers.edu/~jlynch/Writing/

Miscellaneous collection of rules, comments on style and general advice on writing. The author is an associate professor at Rutgers University and specializes in eighteenth century literature.

Quotes

Quotations at Bartleby.com

http://www.bartleby.com/quotations/

Over 80,000 quotations from three different sources. Bartleby.com scores again.

The Quotations Page

http://www.quotationspage.com/

Long-established site with a searchable database containing over 21,000 quotes. You can also browse by subject or author.

BrainyQuote

http://www.brainyquote.com/

Sound intelligent with a smart saying from this collection of 45,000 quotes, organized by topic, author or type.

Mark Twain Quotations

http://www.twainquotes.com/

"The right word may be effective, but no word was ever as effective as a rightly timed pause." Huge collection of quotations from one of the masters of the pithy comment, organized by subject.

Shakespeare Quotes

http://www.allshakespeare.com/quotes/

To be or not to be, friends, Romans, countrymen, in the winter of our discontent. This useful site lists 100 of Shakespeare's most famous lines, then explains which play they come from, which character says them and what is happening at the time.

AltaVista Babel Fish

http://babelfish.altavista.com/

Translate short pieces of text by typing or pasting them into the box, or enter a Web address to translate an entire page. The translations are mechanical, so they aren't 100 per cent accurate, but you can get the gist of an article – and the errors are often amusing. Babel Fish turns Dutch, French, German, Greek, Italian, Spanish, Portuguese, Russian, Chinese, Japanese and Korean into English, and vice versa.

FreeTranslation.com

http://www.freetranslation.com/

FreeTranslation has fewer languages than Babel Fish, but it lets you enter 10,000 characters of text, rather than the 150 words supported by Babel Fish. It's useful for chunks of Dutch, French, German, Italian, Spanish, Portuguese, Russian and Chinese.

Google Language Tools

http://www.google.com/

Follow the Language Tools link from the main page to search for Web pages written in a particular language and translate text or Web pages. You can also use the Google interface in any language from Afrikaans to Zulu, including Hacker, Pig Latin, Klingon and Bork, bork, bork!

Infobel World - Telephone Directories

http://www.infobel.com/world/

This site enables you to search for people and businesses in the UK, the US, Canada and a number of European countries. For other countries, click through to the International section, where it catalogs online telephone directories and related resources for over 180 countries. It includes yellow pages and business directories as well as white pages (residential directories) and has a brief description of each site.

Postal Rates.info

http://www.postalrates.info/

Postal Rates.info does a similar job for postal information, directing you to postal authorities and sites that calculate postage, provide information about stamps and check ZIP codes and postcodes.

Yahoo! People Search

http://people.yahoo.com/

Yahoo!'s People Search enables you to hunt for US and Canadian street addresses or email addresses from anywhere. If you don't find your friends this way, try searching the Web instead – they may have Web pages with their details.

Friends Reunited

http://www.friendsreunited.com/

Friends Reunited lists its members according to their old school, university, workplace, team or club, enabling you to relocate people you've lost touch with over the years. Once you've registered, you can create your own entry and decide whether to contact any of your old buddies. It has services for the UK, Ireland and Eire, Australia, New Zealand, South Africa, Hong Kong, Malaysia and Singapore.

AnyWho

http://www.anywho.com/

AT&T's AnyWho site helps you find people and businesses in the US. There's also a reverse search that turns a phone number into a name and address.

WhitePages.com

http://www.whitepages.com/

Another site that enables you to search for people and businesses in the US and Canada. It also has reverse searches, area codes and ZIP codes. Once you've found someone, you can store their details in an online address book.

United States Postal Service

http://www.usps.com/

Everything you might want to know about sending mail within the US, including a ZIP code finder, a post office locator and information about printing your own postage labels.

BT 118500 Directory Enquiries

http://www.118500.com/

The electronic version of BT's Directory Enquiries service gives you access to the complete UK phone book. Plug in a person's surname and town to find their number, assuming they're in the book. Once you've found an address, you can view a map of the location. You can also search for businesses.

192.com

http://www.192.com/

192.com draws its information from the UK electoral roll, so it can find addresses for people who don't have telephones (or don't have a phone in their name). Once you've got an address, you can find out who lives next door.

Yell.com

http://www.yell.com/

Looking for a plumber in Manchester? Yell.com, the electronic version of the Yellow Pages, lets you search for businesses by location and name or function. It also has a nationwide Film Finder that tells you what's on at your local cinema.

Scoot

http://www.scoot.co.uk/

Scoot is an alternative business directory with similar features to Yell.com, including a Cinema Finder.

Royal Mail

http://www.royalmail.com/

Useful features on the UK's Royal Mail site include postcode and address checkers, a postal calculator and a Track & Trace option that checks the progress of Registered and Recorded Delivery items.

Australian White Pages Online

http://www.whitepages.com.au/wp/

Australia's White Pages are online, enabling you to track down people and businesses. There's also a postcode checker and you can follow the link to the Yellow Pages site for further business listings.

New Zealand White Pages

http://www.whitepages.co.nz/

The Internet White Pages Web site makes it easy to search for people, businesses, doctors and hospitals, and government departments.

Singapore Phone Book

http://www.phonebook.com.sg/

Singapore's online phone book has residential, business and government listings, with a reverse search for business and government numbers. Use the map links to find out where you need to go.

Singapore Post

http://www.singpost.com/

If you have to post a letter, SingPost's site makes it easy: there's a postcode finder, a post office and postbox locator and a table of rates.

Maps and country details

CIA World Factbook

http://www.cia.gov/cia/publications/factbook/

The World Factbook provides basic intelligence about every country in the world. Since it's a publicly available document, it concentrates on the not-so-secret stuff: location, geography, population, government, economy, communication and so on. It's an excellent source of facts and figures.

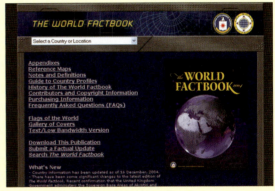

World Gazetteer

http://www.world-gazetteer.com/

If you're specifically interested in people, visit the World Gazetteer to check the population of any country, region or city you care to name. Useful features for impressing friends include a list of the worlds largest metropolitan areas (lead by Tokyo) and cities (topped by Shanghai).

Flags of the World

http://flagspot.net/flags/

Flags of the World is devoted to vexillology (the study of flags). Not content with simply providing a picture of the flag of each country, it offers a wealth of additional details: information about the design and origin, alternative flags, historical flags, marine ensigns, coats of arms and so on.

MapQuest World Atlas

http://www.mapquest.com/atlas/

The MapQuest site has attractive but not especially detailed maps of continents, countries, oceans and polar regions. It's worth a look if you just need a basic outline with major cities.

National Geographic Map Machine

http://plasma.nationalgeographic.com/mapmachine/

Give the Map Machine the name of a place and it'll find you a map. You can then change the theme to see anything from the physical relief or population density to the annual rainfall.

Expedia Maps

http://maps.expedia.com/

Expedia Maps has driving maps of the US and Europe and topographical maps of the entire world. The maps are available in three sizes – small, medium

and large – and zooming in gives you a reasonable amount of detail.

Terraserver

http://www.terraserver.com/

For a different perspective, try the Terraserver, which gives you access to aerial and satellite photography. Coverage isn't complete, but it's still fun to look down on the world.

Multimap

http://www.multimap.com/

Multimap has street maps of the US, the UK and Europe and basic road maps of the rest of the world. Special features include aerial photographs of most of England and Wales.

Streetmap.co.uk

http://www.streetmap.co.uk/

Streetmap has street maps of all of mainland Britain, searchable by street, postcode, place name, grid reference, latitude/longitude and telephone code – so if you know anything at all about the place you're trying to find, it should be able to produce a map. Like Multimap, it has aerial photos of some areas.

RAC

http://www.rac.co.uk/

Once you know where in the UK you're going, use the RAC's routefinder to get there. Simply plug in your current location and destination and it tells you how to drive between them. It even works out how long the journey should take.

Whereis Online

http://www.whereis.com.au/

Whereis doesn't just show you maps of Australian cities, it also tells you how to drive – or walk – from one place to another.

GeoScience Australia

http://www.ga.gov.au/map/

The GeoScience site lets you create your own maps by zooming in on its master map of Australia, then deciding whether you want to display roads, rivers, airports and so on.

The Atlas of Canada

http://atlas.gc.ca/

Lots of maps and facts covering the people, economy, health, environment and climate of Canada. The Map Archives hold many older maps.

Can.com.sg

http://www.can.com.sg/

Select the MapFinder option for an interactive map of Singapore. You can search for almost anything, including streets, postcodes, companies, major buildings and attractions. When you zoom in, the map shows individual buildings.

Clocks and calendars

Timeanddate.com

http://www.timeanddate.com/

Convenient single-page display of the current time in over 250 cities around the world. Alternatively, you can create a customized view showing only the cities where you have friends or colleagues. You can also create a calendar for any month or year.

World Time Server

http://www.worldtimeserver.com/

Attractive world clock that provides the current time in the country or major city of your choice. It can also convert future times to your local time.

Today's Calendar and Clock Page

http://www.ecben.net/calendar.shtml

Although it isn't much to look at, this site catalogs lots of clock and calendar resources. If you're looking for any kind of calendar, be it Julian or Gregorian, Jewish, Islamic or Hindu, you'll find a link here.

Earth Calendar

http://www.earthcalendar.net/

Earth Calendar concentrates on the important dates: holidays, celebrations, anniversaries and gratuitous days off. You can browse the holidays by date, country or religion.

This Day in History

http://www.historychannel.com/tdih/

The History Channel's This Day in History page provides accounts of the major events that occurred on today's date in previous years. You can settle for general history or delve into specific areas such as crime, entertainment and technology. It also has separate sections for major conflicts, from the Civil War to the Cold War.

Moon Phases

http://www.googol.com/moon/

Attractive site that provides a visual calendar of the phases of the moon, for any month of any year.

Earth and Moon Viewer

http://www.fourmilab.ch/earthview/vplanet.html

Entertaining tool/toy that creates simulated views of the Earth and Moon at the current moment, showing you the areas of daylight and darkness.

Numbers and measurements

A Dictionary of Units

http://www.projects.ex.ac.uk/trol/dictunit/

A Dictionary of Units has lots of information about measurements, units, the Systeme International (SI) and metrification, plus a comprehensive set of convertors that take the strain off your brain.

The NIST Reference on Constants, Units and Uncertainty

http://physics.nist.gov/cuu/

NIST is the (US) National Institute of Science and Technology. On this unfortunately named but nicely designed site it provides values for the fundamental physical constants, a thorough explanation of the Systeme International (SI) units and some notes about uncertainty.

WebElements Periodic Table

http://www.webelements.com/

Excellent resource for students and chemists, with information about all the elements – including photographs, cartoons and comments such as, "The most romantic way to extract gold is by panning it out from a stream in some pleasant valley but most such sources are now depleted." It comes in both professional and scholar editions – the pro version has more details.

FirstGov

http://www.firstgov.gov/

Your first port of call for information from the US Government, be it straightforward advice about birth certificates and voting or obscure details such as the current wait times at border crossing-points.

White House

http://www.whitehouse.gov/

Take a virtual tour of the US President's des res or find out about his activities and policies. The Vice President and First Lady get their own sections and kids can read about the President's pets.

Government of Canada

http://canada.gc.ca/

Well-organized site with government information for Canadians, non-Canadians (visitors and potential immigrants) and businesses.

Directgov

http://www.direct.gov.uk/

Starting point for accessing UK government and public-service Web sites. Mostly you'll click on to other places, but you can also get advice on everything from having a baby to death and bereavement.

10 Downing Street

http://www.number-10.gov.uk/

Not to be outdone by the Americans, the UK Prime Minister also has a home in cyberspace, complete with panoramic images of his home. Once you've admired the decor, you can read the press briefings, watch videos of Prime Minister's Question Time and browse assorted fact files.

australia.gov.au

http://www.australia.gov.au/

Another country, another portal that serves primarily to bounce you off to other sites. It has sections for Australians, businesses and nonresidents, making it easy to access appropriate information. You'll also find information about Australia and its government.

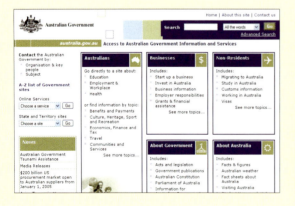

govt.nz

http://www.govt.nz/

This Web site catalogs government and council information alphabetically, by type and by life event. You can also find out how to request information from an MP or government organization or provide feedback on issues currently under debate.

SINGOV

http://www.gov.sg/

Singapore's SINGOV catalogs government services and keeps you informed about statements and speeches. You can get a daily summary by email.

South Africa Government Online

http://www.gov.za/

This site is divided into two main areas, for services and information. You'll find advice for people, organizations and foreign nationals and you can download government forms.

Science and Technology

The great paradox of the Internet is that all the information you need to get connected is available online… but you can't access it until you've got your computer connected. By then you'll be interested in other things: finding Web sites, choosing new software and hardware, and laughing at geek humor. Fortunately there's loads of advice on these subjects as well.

Finding Web sites

Search Engine Watch

http://searchenginewatch.com/

Search Engine Watch lists and reviews search engines and provides advice on hunting for sites. The section on the major search engines, with descriptions of their features, is handy for beginners. Specialist and multimedia search engines are listed separately.

Google

http://www.google.com/

The critic's favorite, thanks to a clean interface and the ability to magic up relevant results. It also offers specialist image, newsgroup, news and shopping searches, plus a Web directory. With so much on offer here, there's little reason to look elsewhere.

Yahoo!

http://www.yahoo.com/

Yahoo! was one of the first really popular Web sites. It still gets many visitors today, although they come as much for its other offerings – Web-based email, instant messaging and so on – as for the directory that started it all off. It's still worth a look when you're researching a broad area and just want the best sites. Localized versions cater to specific countries and regions, including the UK & Ireland, Canada, Australia & NZ and Singapore.

AltaVista

http://www.altavista.com/

AltaVista was once the Web's leading search engine, but its popularity slipped when it diversified into other areas. Today the focus is back on searching, with general, image, MP3/audio, video and news searches. Numerous localized versions enable you to restrict your search to sites from a specific country.

MSN Search

http://search.msn.com/

MSN lets you search the Web or look for images or news stories. You can flip between different types of searches simply by clicking the links at the top of the results page.

Excite

http://www.excite.com/

Like Yahoo!, Excite now offers so many extra features, from news and stock prices to personal horoscopes, that it's easy to miss the Search box in the middle of the page. You can search the entire Web or just Excite's directory, or look for photos.

Lycos

http://www.lycos.com/

Lycos offers Web, news, shopping and picture searches, plus a range of other services.

Ask Jeeves

http://www.ask.com/

Ask Jeeves responds to plain-English questions, saving you the bother of posing your query in computer-speak.

Web Wombat

http://www.webwombat.com.au/

Web Wombat is an Aussie search engine cum directory cum portal site with news, weather, horoscopes and so on. It's useful if you're specifically interested in Australian Web sites.

LookSmart

http://search.looksmart.com/

LookSmart offers a searchable, categorized directory of Web sites with brief comments from the LookSmart reviewers. There's also a general Web Search and a Find Articles option that searches over 900 publications.

Yahoo! Daily Picks

http://picks.yahoo.com/

If you're looking for something new or topical, Yahoo!'s Daily Picks section highlights recent additions to the directory and sites worth seeing. A good choice for a rainy afternoon.

Netsurfer Digest

http://www.netsurf.com/nsd/

Netsurfer Digest is an e-zine (electronic magazine) that highlights topical Web sites and Internet trends. Sadly, you now have to pay an annual subscription to receive the weekly bulletins. Offshoots deal with science, education, books and robotics.

Encyclopedias

PC Webopaedia

http://www.pcwebopaedia.com/

Look up those mysterious technical terms in the PC Webopaedia, an online dictionary that not only provides explanations but also gives you links to sites where you can explore the subject in more detail. A list of the top 15 search terms lets you see what's puzzling other Internet users.

Whatis?com

http://whatis.techtarget.com/

If you're still mystified, try Whatis?com, a slightly geekier dictionary that covers some of the more obscure computing terms.

NetLingo

http://www.netlingo.com/

NetLingo is an Internet dictionary that explains all the strange terms that are used online. Find out what is meant by "cornea gumbo", "kevorking" and "meatspace". It also has a collection of smileys – little faces made out of keyboard characters.

PC Technology Guide

http://www.pctechguide.com/

The PC Technology Guide concentrates on the stuff inside (and attached to) your system box. If you're been baffled by a sales assistant or just want to know how your computer works, this is the place to start. It begins gently but gets quite technical.

General computing

CNET.com

http://www.cnet.com/

Vast site with technology news, features, product reviews, software to download and advice for Web designers. It was easier to find your way around when the site was smaller and less successful, but there's plenty here that's worth reading. Reviewers are clear about their likes and dislikes and there's some useful material for beginners… somewhere.

ZDnet

http://www.zdnet.com/

Technically part of the CNET Network, ZDNet still feels separate and different. Like CNET.com, it has news, features, reviews and a download library, but it offers more depth and weight. Watch out for the buyers' guides, which explain what to look for in your new toys.

MaxPC

http://www.maxpc.co.uk/

MaxPC collates reviews, features and tutorials from the computer magazines produced by Future Publishing, a UK-based company. You can also click through to the sites of the individual titles for a more focused approach.

Computer Buyer

http://www.computerbuyer.co.uk/

Produced by the UK magazine of the same name, the Computer Buyer site succeeds where so many others fail: it's easy to navigate. Start with the latest news, reviews and features, then plunge into the archives, which integrate material from sister titles *Computer Shopper, PC Pro and MacUser.*

The Register

http://www.theregister.co.uk/

The Register is a UK-based news site that offers opinionated reports on the latest developments in computing. Its willingness to snipe at anyone and everyone (the site's tag line is, "Biting the hand that feeds IT") makes it more readable than the average technology site.

Australian PC World

http://pcworld.idg.com.au/

The PC World site has the usual mixture of news, reviews and features, but with an Australian twist.

Highlights include the Buying Guides, which cover everything from motherboards to antivirus software, and the HelpScreen section, where you can post a problem and get help from other readers and the magazine's staff.

Internet

Wired News

http://www.wired.com/news/

The latest on the Internet, in fluorescent colors, from the iconoclastic *Wired* magazine. It's easier on the eye than the printed version, because the wild colors are pushed off into the margins, and it has the most interesting stories. Always worth a look, especially if you have a penchant for the offbeat.

.net

http://www.netmag.co.uk/

UK Internet magazine *.net* covers the Internet from an ordinary user's point of view. Highlights of its site include the In-depth Articles section, which is packed with features from previous issues of the printed magazine, and the Web Builder section, which helps you create your own Web site.

Web User

http://www.webuser.co.uk/

Another UK-based Internet magazine, with news, product and Web-site reviews, and forums for discussing Internet issues. The Broadband Price Guide provides an overview of broadband services.

All About the Internet

http://www.isoc.org/internet/

Dry, minimalist guide from the Internet Society. It concentrates on Internet law and is mostly of interest for its links to other sites, which include several histories of the Net.

AARP Computers & Technology

http://www.aarp.org/learntech/computers/

AARP, the American Associated for Retired People, provides a not-too-technical guide to computers and the Internet. Special features include a set of seven Basic Web Lessons that explain how to start surfing. Once you've mastered all seven, you can move on to the five Intermediate Web Lessons.

Internet Tutorials

http://library.albany.edu/internet/

These online tutorials from the University at Albany Library start with the basics and then provide in-depth advice on using the Web for research. Worth a look if you're a student, teacher or academic.

Webmonkey

http://webmonkey.wired.com/webmonkey/

Learn how to build your own Web site with material from *Wired* magazine. Separate introductions for beginners, builders and masters help you find appropriate tutorials and advice. As well as the "how to" material it has a Quick Reference section with HTML tags, special characters, color codes, a JavaScript library and a Stylesheet guide.

Hardware

Intel

http://www.intel.com/

Find out what makes your computer tick, compare your processor with Intel's latest and greatest offering and see what else the company is up to. You can even take a virtual tour of the Intel museum. Intel also has localized Web pages for many countries.

IBM

http://www.ibm.com/

Like most manufacturers, the inventor of the PC doesn't just tout its new computers online, it also helps you keep your current one in shape. Visit the Support and Downloads section for solutions to your technical problems and updated drivers.

Dell

http://www.dell.com/

Dell sells over the Internet in many countries – select yours from the drop-down list. Find out what's available and specify the system of your dreams, without grappling with pushy salespeople.

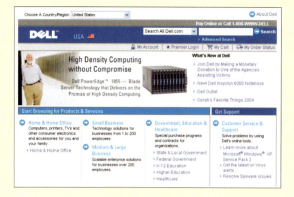

Hewlett-Packard

http://www.hp.com/

HP makes everything from desktop computers to printers, scanners and digital cameras, so its site doesn't just sell you individual products, it also shows you how they all fit together. It has local sites for many countries, but is inclined to flip you back to the US site when you request more information.

Apple

http://www.apple.com/

Think different(ly) at Apple's site, which attempts to lure you away from the Windows world with information about its friendly and stylish computers. This is also the place to get information about the ubiquitous iPod, along with software products such as iTunes and QuickTime.

Epson

http://www.epson.com/

Epson's well-organized sites provide lots of information about its printers and scanners. They also help you make the most of them with downloadable software and online problem solvers. In the UK, check out the Photo Expert site (http://www.photoexpert.epson.co.uk/) for advice on digital imaging.

Scantips

http://www.scantips.com/

Having problems getting pictures on to your computer? This site provides reams of information on scanners, scanner software and scanning. Detailed explanations of concepts such as resolution are followed by advice on the settings to choose and tips for improving the results.

Iomega

http://www.iomega.com/

Iomega's sites provide information about its myriad different drives – including Zip, CD-RW, hard and Mini USB – and help you choose one. Depending on your location, you may be able to purchase it online. You can also download the latest version of the drive software and sometimes you'll find fun activities such as games and competitions.

USRobotics

http://www.usr.com/

Check out the latest modems from USRobotics and learn more about the technologies they use. You can also download drivers, upgrades, data sheets, manuals and troubleshooting guides.

Zoom Telephonics

http://www.zoom.com/

Find out about Zoom's extensive range of broadband and dial-up modems or get technical support for your current hardware.

Curt's High-speed Modem FAQ

http://www.net-boy.com/

If you want to know how your modem works (or why it isn't working), Curt's page is a good place to start. It explains everything from connection speeds to the ins and outs of 56kbps technology and software

modems. It's particularly helpful when you're trying to achieve a happy relationship between an older computer and an older modem.

Logitech

http://www.logitech.com/

Input specialist Logitech sells mice, keyboards and Webcams. Its stylish site has all the details and makes it easy to compare products.

Typing Injury FAQ

http://www.tifaq.com/

Sore hands? Aching wrists? The Typing Injury FAQ advises you on the proper arrangement of your desk, chair, keyboard and screen. It also covers alternative keyboards and pointing devices.

Creative

http://www.creative.com/

Although it's best known for the Sound Blaster range of sound cards, Singapore-based Creative also produces MP3 players, speakers, graphics cards and many other multimedia add-ons.

Palm

http://www.palmone.com/

Is that a handheld in your pocket, or are you just pleased to see me? Admire the latest Palms, inspect the accessories and stock up on software.

Microsoft

http://www.microsoft.com/

A gigantic site for a titan among companies. Here you will (eventually) find information about all Microsoft's products and programs. If one of your applications is misbehaving, go to the Support section and search the Knowledge Base, a huge database of reported problems and their solutions. You can also visit Bill Gates' personal home page and try to divine the secrets of his success.

Linux

http://www.linux.com/

Linux is an alternative operating system that can be used in place of Windows. Linux.com provides news and information, an introduction for beginners and links to relevant Web sites. The associated Freshmeat Web site (http://freshmeat.net/) catalogs Linux software.

LinuxQuestions.org

http://www.linuxquestions.org/

You've got Linux… so now what? Post your questions in the forums on this site and get advice from other Linux users. Topic areas include software, hardware, networking and security.

Adobe

http://www.adobe.com/

Adobe's professional graphics and design programs include Photoshop, Illustrator, PageMaker, GoLive and Premier. Find out more about them, download tryout versions and upgrades, and get tips and advice. This is also the place to come if you need a copy of Adobe Reader to display PDF files.

Corel

http://www.corel.com/

Corel produces two big-name applications – CorelDraw Graphics Suite and WordPerfect Office – plus a number of less familiar ones, including the "looks like real artwork" painting program CorelPainter. Its Web site has product information, trial versions, updates and a database of questions and answers. Visit the Community areas for tutorials, tips and tricks, and templates.

Macromedia

http://www.macromedia.com/

On the Internet, Macromedia is best known as the producer of Flash Player and Shockwave Player. In the real world, it produces a range of graphics and Web-design programs, including Dreamweaver, Macromedia Flash (the program used to create Flash animations), Director and FreeHand.

Jasc

http://www.jasc.com/

Jasc (now owned by Corel) is best known for Paint Shop Pro, which is available from this site as a trial version or to purchase and download. You can also download freebies and work through the tutorials in its Learning Center, which covers digital photography, Web design and computer art.

Symantec

http://www.symantec.com/

Symantec produces software that protects and optimizes your computer, including antivirus programs and the perennially popular Norton Utilities. If you have a broadband connection, you can purchase the programs online and download them to your hard disk. Visit the Security Response section for details of the latest virus threats.

Mozilla

http://www.mozilla.org/

Mozilla is attempting to break Microsoft's stranglehold on the Internet with new Web browser Firefox and email program Thunderbird. Download them both from this site.

Nullsoft

http://www.winamp.com/

Join the MP3 generation by downloading Nullsoft's popular Winamp player. The Web site also has music, music videos, a huge library of skins (add-ons that change Winamp's appearance), a llama and a load of laid-back humor.

Tucows

http://www.tucows.com/

Blown your software budget already? Visit Tucows for over 40,000 freeware and shareware programs, themes, skins and screensavers. The search engine lets you specify your operating system and the programs have brief descriptions and ratings.

Simtel

http://www.simtel.net/

Another shareware and freeware library. The Featured Downloads area highlights the best programs and there's an intriguing Top 100 list that shows you what other people are downloading.

Download.com

http://www.download.com/

Brought to you by CNET Networks, this site has all manner of downloadable software, from demos of commercial programs to shareware and freeware. There's plenty of information and you can browse by program type or search for specific applications.

Screensaver.com

http://www.screensaver.com/

Download Windows eye candy from this site, which not only features screen savers but also desktop themes – coordinated wallpapers, icons, cursors and sounds. Some are free, others are shareware.

1001 Free Fonts

http://www.1001fonts.com/

If you can get past the intrusive advertising, this site has free fonts for Windows and Mac, sorted by style: calligraphic, decorative, dingbat, graffiti, hard to read, retro and so on.

Computer games

Happy Puppy

http://www.happypuppy.com/

Long-standing games site that covers all the major platforms, from humble handhelds to shiny PS2s

and Xboxes. As well as news, reviews and features for avid gamers, it has downloadable demos, trailers, patches, mods and tools.

Gamespot

http://www.gamespot.com/

Very busy and professional site with news, reviews, previews, demos, patches, tips, articles, interviews… everything a gamer could desire, for all the major platforms. You'll need to pay an annual subscription to access all the material, but there's no shortage of free content if you're broke.

PC Gamer

http://www.pcgamer.com/

The Web site of "the world's best-selling PC games magazine" has game reviews and a chart of the top 50 demos. They're available for download, although you'll want a fast connection.

id Software

http://www.idsoftware.com/

Visit the home of Wolfenstein, Doom and Quake, the first-person shoot-'em-ups that have rampaged round the globe, bringing terms such as "frag" and "bfg" to previously sedate offices. id's site has the lowdown on all its games, from its very first efforts (anyone remember Commander Keen?) to its latest blockbusters, with demos and updates for the more recent titles.

Electronic Arts

http://www.ea.com/

EA publishes gazillions of games for PC, PlayStation, Nintendo and Xbox. Titles you've probably heard of include Sim City and The Sims, Need for Speed and Command & Conquer. It also produces film tie-ins for the likes of the James Bond and Harry Potter movies and sports games featuring everything from football and basketball to snowmobile racing.

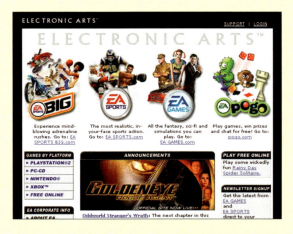

Sierra

http://www.sierra.com/

Sierra's titles range from the explosive Half-Life to the family-friendly Incredible Machine. Most games have their own Web sites, which you can reach from the Sierra home page.

LucasArts

http://www.lucasarts.com/

Get your *Star Wars* games here, basically. LucasArts makes the odd diversion into other areas with the likes of Indiana Jones games and the destructive Mercenaries, but *Star Wars* spin-offs dominate its range. If you're struggling, visit the Support section and put your questions to Yoda.

PlayStation

http://www.playstation.com/

The PlayStation Web site has news, game details, hardware specifications and forums, all wrapped up in an animated interface.

Xbox

http://www.xbox.com/

Find out what's happening with Xbox hardware and games, then visit the Xbox Live section to learn how to play games over the Internet. There's also a community area where you can chat about specific games or general Xbox issues.

ClassicGaming

http://www.classicgaming.com/

Hankering after the games of your youth? This site explains how to install an emulator and relive the days of the Amstrad CPC, Atari 2600, Apple II and Commodore 64. It also has many arcade games.

Geek things

Complete Guide to Cows

http://userpages.umbc.edu/~dschmil/text/cow-list.txt

Why settle for a smiley face made out of keyboard characters when you could have a cow? These cows are ASCII art, the only way to add pictures to your email in the early days of the Internet.

Hamster Dance

http://www.hampsterdance.com/

Very annoying animated hamsters that bop round to a very annoying tune. One of the more inexplicable Internet fads.

I Kiss You

http://www.ikissyou.org/

The Mahir Cagri phenomenon can't be explained, it simply has to be experienced. This site collects together Mahir-related material, from parodies and games to press articles and links to fan sites. It also provides some background on the amiable Turk who became an Internet celebrity, but don't expect to be much the wiser after reading it.

Dancing baby

http://www.dancing-baby.net/

Take a computer model of a baby, superimpose a cha-cha motion and this is what you get – a surreal animation that toured the Internet and then took on a life of its own. There are all sorts of dancing babies out there now, but this site has the original file.

All Your Base

http://www.planettribes.com/allyourbase/

In the beginning, there was a video game. And the introduction was translated into English, very badly, producing the phrase, "All your base are belong to us," which then reappeared on signs, in magazines and adverts, on computers and in other strange places. What does it mean? Nobody knows.

Stick Figure Death Theater

http://www.sfdt.com/

Tasteless but blackly humorous, Stick Figure Death Theater is a collection of crudely drawn animations in which people come to sticky ends. There are no surprises – the stick figure always ends up in a pool of red pixels – but it's compulsive viewing.

Eric Conveys an Emotion

http://www.emotioneric.com/ae/

Eric has a camera. Eric acts out his emotions, on camera, and displays the pictures on the Web. In the Adventure Edition, he develops his theme into strip cartoons, with unpredictable events provoking some unusual expressions.

Science

New Scientist.com

http://www.newscientist.com/

The Web site of *New Scientist* magazine has news and articles, as you might expect. Less predictable material includes The Last Word, a collection of questions about everyday phenomena such as dripping taps and nodding pigeons. There's also a huge directory of recommended science Web sites with detailed write-ups.

Scientific American

http://www.sciam.com/

More science news and features, plus weekly polls and an opportunity to put your questions to the experts. Nanotechnology gets a section of its own, so this a good place to come if you're interested in "a vast grab bag of stuff that has to do with creating tiny things that sometimes just happen to be useful". Bring your magnifying glass.

Discovery

http://www.discovery.com/

The Web site of the Discovery Channel (and its many spin-offs) supplements its programs with multimedia and interactive features. You rarely just read anything – there's almost always something to do, whether it's diving in a virtual submarine, building your own dinosaur, exploring the space station or monitoring the polar bear cam.

Scientific American Frontiers

http://www.pbs.org/saf/

The *Scientific American Frontiers* site doesn't just tell you about the series of science specials hosted by Alan Alda, it enables you to watch them over the Internet. There's hours (literally) of intriguing entertainment here.

HowStuffWorks

http://www.howstuffworks.com/

Excellent and very popular site that does exactly what it says in the title bar: it explains how stuff works. By "stuff" it means everything from car engines and computers to tattoos, caffeine and Christmas. The articles are clear and entertaining, with lots of cross references and links to other relevant Web sites.

Bill Nye.com

http://www.billnye.com/

Bill Nye the Science Guy has a sophisticated site with experiments to try at home, miscellaneous interesting facts and a question of the week. The experiments ("demos" in Nye-speak) use everyday household items and don't seem likely to cause cataclysmic explosions in your kitchen.

Animal Diversity Web

http://animaldiversity.ummz.umich.edu/

The Animal Diversity Web has thousands of articles about animal species, written by university students. They are sorted into a proper taxonomic hierarchy, but you can use the search engine to skip all the Latin and go straight to a page on your favorite beast. As the all-inclusive title suggests, it covers everything from creepy-crawlies to lions, tigers and elephants.

BBC Science & Nature

http://www.bbc.co.uk/sn/

Lots more natural history from the BBC, including a Wildfacts database covering hundreds of animals, a special section on British wildlife, features about pets, live Webcams, electronic postcards and information about all its nature programs.

The Why Files

http://whyfiles.org/

The Why Files explains the science behind the news, in detail but without using too many big words. Accessible and even humorous, it adds a new feature every week. The front page also points you back to stories that are relevant to this week's events and you can browse the archive by topic or search for particular subjects.

Physics Central

http://www.physicscentral.com/

$E=mc^2$ and all that. This whiz-bang Web site is brought to you by the American Physics Society and has sections for physics in action, people in physics, physics pictures and physics news. The authors attempt to keep everything on a layperson's plane, although the odd technical term creeps in.

NASA

http://www.nasa.gov/

Start here for all things astronomical, astronautical or otherwise space-related, then click through to the space agency's many dynamic subsites. The Human Space Flight site (http://spaceflight.nasa.gov/) is the highlight, with information about every manned flight from the first Mercury mission to the latest Shuttle and Space Station adventures.

Space.com

http://www.space.com/

When you get done at NASA's site, Space.com promises "something amazing every day". It has space news, science and astronomy features and a Space Views section with image galleries, desktop wallpaper, screensavers and electronic postcards. The NightSky section tells you what to look for if you're outside on a clear night this week.

A.L.I.C.E. AI Foundation

http://www.alicebot.org/

Chat with A.L.I.C.E., twice the winner of the Loebner Prize for artificial intelligence. To win, the chatterbot had to sustain a typed conversation with the judges. Only one person confused "her" with a human, and once you've indulged in a surreal conversation with the artificial entity, you'll realize "she" still needs to work on her social skills.

Robots.net

http://robots.net/

Useful resource for robotics enthusiasts, with links to articles from around the Web and a Robomenu where you can show off your creations.

Entertainment

As well as being entertaining in its own right, the Internet also has lots of information about real-world amusements. Find out about the latest movies, check up on the music world, see what's on the box, read about books, view art and find something to laugh about.

What's on

Whatsonwhen.com

http://www.whatsonwhen.com/

What's on. And when. And where, which is just as important, especially given that this site covers the globe. If you're feeling practical, choose your country or city (or the place you're about to visit). Those with money to burn can pick a theme and a date, then call their travel agents with instructions.

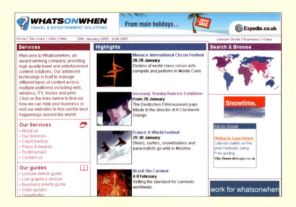

Festivals.com

http://www.festivals.com/

Festivals.com catalogs festivals and celebrations around the globe. It has subsections for arts, kids, motor, music, sports and cultural events, with features to get you enthused before you peruse the listings. You can also search for events by country.

Time Out

http://www.timeout.com/

The *Time Out* Web site has guides to over 90 cities, with reviews of restaurants, bars, cafés, hotels and stores, plus a roundup of the month's events. If you're still stuck for something to do, follow the links to local Web sites for each city.

Ticketmaster

http://www.ticketmaster.com/

Ticketmaster sells tickets for concerts, shows and sporting events in North America, the UK, Ireland, Scandinavia, Australia, Brazil and Chile. Events are sorted into categories and the most popular ones are highlighted. Listings have information about both the event and the venue, including seating plans, and you can purchase tickets online.

Aloud.com

http://www.aloud.com/

Aloud.com sells tickets for gigs, concerts and festivals. You can search by artist, location or genre, but you have to know what you want to see because there's no information about the events. An online ticket tracker helps you find out what has happened to your precious scraps of paper.

Ticketek.com

http://www.ticketek.com/

Ticketek covers Australia, New Zealand and Argentina. It sells tickets for concerts, performances, sporting events and festivals and provides information about both the events and the venues. Tickets can be purchased online. In Australia, you can even purchase electronic tickets for some events – instead of queuing up at the box office, you print your own ticket.

Sistic

http://www.sistic.com.sg/

Sistic sells tickets for events taking place in Singapore. You can search by event name, venue or month, or browse the categorized listings.

Artslink.co.za

http://www.artslink.co.za/

Artslink.co.za has daily arts news, a weekly guide to the South African arts scene and a calendar of festivals and annual events.

Computicket

http://www.computicket.com/

South Africa's Computicket site sells tickets for the cinema, theatre, live events and sport. You can also buy bus tickets – handy if you need to travel.

Entertainment Weekly

http://www.ew.com/ew/

Like the magazine, the *Entertainment Weekly* Web site has something for everyone. It covers movies, videos, DVDs, television, music, books and popular culture. Check out the box office and television charts to find out what Americans are watching and test your hipness with the pop quizzes.

People.com

http://people.aol.com/people/

People.com deals with the famous and the beautiful. It has lots of profiles and photographs, a fashion section and a rundown of the top star couplings and uncouplings of the year.

E! Online

http://www.eonline.com/

E! Online is entertaining about the entertainment scene, with smartly presented news, features, reviews and gossip. Don't miss the Fun section, where you'll find gems such as the 'N Sync-erator, a tricky jigsaw puzzle that requires you to distinguish one member of the boy band from another.

Metacritic

http://www.metacritic.com/

Metacritic collects film, video/DVD, music, game and book reviews, then compiles them into a single metareview with an overall score. You can read a quick quote from each of the reviewers or click through to the original review for the full story. A smart idea, executed well.

Movies

Internet Movie Database

http://www.imdb.com/

The Internet Movie Database (IMDb) is the definitive movie Web site. Here you'll find everything your movie-loving heart desires, from cast lists and synopses to trivia and goofs to links to reviews from all around the Web. It also covers television, although not with quite the same attention to every minor detail.

Ain't It Cool News

http://www.aintitcool.com/

Obsession takes another form at Ain't It Cool News, where the redheaded Harry Knowles dishes the dirt on Hollywood. This is where you'll find rumors about scripts, comments from test screenings and stills from yet-to-be-released movies, bundled up with Harry's take-no-prisoners commentary and LOTS OF CAPITAL LETTERS!!!

Leonard Maltin's Movie Crazy

http://www.leonardmaltin.com/

At the opposite end of the spectrum, well-known movie critic Leonard Maltin offers measured opinions on new movies and DVDs. His journal offers further commentary on the movie business and he includes some personal photographs.

Hollywood.com

http://www.hollywood.com/

US movie site with news, features, reviews and trailers. There's a calendar showing the movies that are due out over the next few months, a Top 10 list of recommended movies and a box-office chart. Check out the Celebs section for photos, interviews, premieres, news and gossip.

Movies.com

http://movies.go.com/

More movie news, more reviews. If you don't feel like reading, you can listen to audio reviews by Robert Ebert and Richard Roeper. Other interesting features include the Buzz Bin, which lists the 20 hottest upcoming movies.

Premiere

http://www.premiere.com/

US movie magazine *Premiere* concentrates on reviews of films and DVDs. There's also a collection of features and a daily poll. Are there too many awards shows? Yes, said 54 per cent of visitors. If you disagree with anything, gripe in the forums.

Film Unlimited

http://film.guardian.co.uk/

The Guardian's movie site has the usual news and reviews, plus interviews (and interview transcripts)

and a Brits in Film section with brief biographies. Fun features include a Mood Matcher that selects movies for such occasions as, "When you're learning to drive," and, "When the planet's being invaded." The Games section has lighthearted quizzes.

Empire Online

http://www.empireonline.co.uk/

Popular British movie mag *Empire* has a vast Web site with lots of reviews, a Future Films section that tracks the progress of the most eagerly awaited movies and a set of buying guides that help you fill out your DVD collection. Premieres get in-depth coverage and you can relive the highs and lows of recent years with its annual reviews.

Miramax Cafe

http://www.miramax.com/

These days if it doesn't have a Web site, it isn't really a movie. The Miramax site provides easy access to information about the movies it is distributing. Each movie gets brief cast and crew details and a synopsis. You can usually view the trailer as well.

Fox Movies.com

http://www.foxmovies.com/

Despite being saddled with a name that looks more dated every year, 20th Century Fox is alive and well and making movies. Find out what's in cinemas, what's being promoted online and what's coming soon. If you're feeling nostalgic, use the Past Favorites section to track down the archived official sites of previous blockbusters.

Dreamworks SKG

http://www.dreamworks.com/

Watch the trailers for Dreamworks movies and find out what's coming out on DVD and video. The studio seems to put almost as much effort into its Web sites as it does into its movies, so expect lots of animated presentations and special effects.

Walt Disney Pictures

http://disney.go.com/disneypictures/

Find out what's coming next from Disney, then extend the movie experience with online games and screensavers. You can also go behind the scenes with the Movie Surfers, a team of young film fans.

QuickTime Movie Trailers

http://www.apple.com/trailers/

There are lots of sites with movie trailers, but this is the best option when you want to cut to the chase. It just lists the trailers by studio, then lets you play them. Most come in several sizes, so you can choose something appropriate to your connection speed.

Drew's Script-O-Rama

http://www.script-o-rama.com/

Find out what your favorite character actually said with Drew's Script-O-Rama, which links you to scripts and transcripts from around the Web. If you can't face all those words, try the Haiku page for the short versions of popular movies.

Oscar.com

http://www.oscar.com/

The official site of the Academy Awards has everything you love about the Oscars – the movies, the frocks, the small gold men – and everything you hate – including the speeches. Come here first when you're looking for nominations or results.

Sundance

http://www.sundance.org/

Start here for the official sites of both the movie-making institute and the festival. Some features are specially modified for wireless browsing from a palmtop computer.

Music Newswire

http://www.vh1.com/news/newswire/

VH1's newswire brings you the top stories, features and reviews from the top music news sites around the Web. It's a convenient one-stop shop for the latest in pop.

Ultimate Band List

http://ubl.artistdirect.com/

Everything you ever wanted to know about every band in the world… probably. Read a brief account of your favorite solo artist or group, peruse their greatest (and not so greatest) albums, listen to songs and follow the links to official and unofficial Web sites. It also lists related artists, although you have to work out the relationships yourself.

MTV.com

http://www.mtv.com/

Like the television channel, MTV.com brings you popular music, 24 hours a day. There's music to download, videos to watch and a fantasy music game to play, plus music news and a database of bands. You can also get the lowdown on shows such as *Celebrity Deathmatch* and *The Osbournes*.

Rolling Stone

http://www.rollingstone.com/

Rolling Stone's Web site feels very much like a magazine, with all the current features and reviews listed on the front page and everything else stored neatly in categorized archives. The distinctive and magazine-ish page layout also sets the site apart and makes the articles easy to read. Don't miss the Photos section, which has lots of stylish images.

LAUNCH

http://uk.launch.yahoo.com/

What was once dotmusic is now LAUNCH, Yahoo!'s UK-based electronic music magazine. It still has news, reviews, features and interviews, plus official charts with commentary and sound clips. You can also listen over the Internet with LAUNCHCast radio.

Q4music.com

http://www.q4music.com/

Although it sounds like a place where you can join a long line of people waiting for free CDs or concert tickets, Q4music.com is actually the online edition of the UK's Q magazine. Novelty features include polls, a Listomania section with essential dozens and celebrity record collections and a Ringtones area that lets you arm your cell phone with annoying electronic versions of the latest hits.

NoiZyland

http://www.noizyland.com/

NoiZyland covers the New Zealand indie music scene. It also has a large collection of links to other New Zealand music sites, so it's a good place to start even if your tastes run more to jazz or classical. The Reviews and Interviews sections catalog all the material published about New Zealand artists, with links to the source Web sites.

BBC Radio 1

http://www.bbc.co.uk/radio1/

Check out the Official UK Top 40 Singles Chart, then listen to the entire countdown over the Internet. You can listen to other Radio 1 shows, too – at your convenience rather than in their normal time slots – and a selection of documentaries. The One Music section has advice for aspiring musos.

Undercover

http://www.undercover.com.au/

Undercover is an Australian music site that combines news, video interviews, reviews and music features. The Tour Guide tells you who's playing where over the next few months and there's a Freebies section where you can win albums, DVDs and concert tickets.

Vivamusic.com

http://www.vivamusic.com/

Vivamusic.com covers the Asian music market, with separate sections for pop, j-pop, dance, k-pop, South East Asian music and others (classical, jazz, new age and so on). It also covers events taking place in its real-world store/venue in Singapore.

Essentials of Music

http://www.essentialsofmusic.com/

Start getting your head around classical music with the Essentials of Music site, which is built around Sony's Essential Classics series of discs. The site provides overviews of the six main eras of music.

Classical Net

http://www.classical.net/

Unattractive but informative site with over 3,000 reviews, advice on building a collection of classical music and links to 4,000 other classical music sites.

Jazz Online

http://www.jazzonline.com/

Long-standing jazz site with reviews, artist Q&As and a Jazz 101 section that introduces the main styles and recommends discs.

SOHH.com

http://www.sohh.com/

SOHH.com specializes in hip hop. Check out The Wire for the latest news, or The Core for in-depth articles. It also has forums where you can rant, rap and generally express your opinions.

MP3.com

http://www.mp3.com/

MP3.com introduces you to the world of MP3 music with software and hardware guides and features. Album reviews include links to sites where you can purchase and download digital versions of the tracks. You can also listen to new albums.

Television

TV Guide Online

http://www.tvguide.com/

The TV Guide site has listings for North American and assorted Central and South American countries, plus news, gossip, features and daily updates on the big American soaps. The ShowGuide section covers hundreds of programs (including programs produced outside the US), with overviews, episode guides and links to features and old cover images. If there's still something you want to know, email your question to the Televisionary.

TV Land

http://www.tvland.com/

TVLand is a funky site covering classic American shows such as *All In The Family*, *The Brady Bunch* and *Taxi*. You'll find episode guides, details of the actors and characters, and sounds and pictures. The site also has theme tunes, games, interviews with TV legends and assorted strangeness.

Television Without Pity

http://www.televisionwithoutpity.com/

Television Without Pity (TWoP to its friends) provides biting recaps of popular US shows such as *Alias*, *CSI*, *Six Feet Under* and *The West Wing*. Part episode guide and part review, the recaps are often funnier than the programs themselves.

TV Tome

http://tvtome.com/

Find out what you missed with episode guides for hundreds of shows, both current and long-forgotten. Plot summaries are brief but you get the general gist of each episode. It also has cast and crew details, trivia and reviews of some episodes.

BBC

http://www.bbc.co.uk/

The BBC's Web site is organized by topic: Business & Money, Children's, Education, Entertainment

and so on. There's also an A-Z that enables you to go straight to the page for your favorite show. There's an enormous amount of everything here, from character guides and video clips to online games, recipes and instructions for decorating your home. If the BBC makes a program about it, there'll be information here.

Channel 4

http://www.channel4.co.uk/

The UK's Channel 4 can't compete with the BBC, but it makes a valiant effort, providing online support for its own shows and also for the programs it imports. Get the word on everything from the lowbrow *Big Brother* to *The Simpsons* and *Desperate Housewives*. If you'd rather work in television than watch it, click through to ideasfactory (http://www.ideasfactory.com/).

thecustard.tv

http://www.thecustard.tv/

Thecustard.tv is an independent site aimed at "young, intelligent, selective television viewers". It lists the programs that are worth watching, day by day, with Top Ten lists for people who can't be bothered to make their own choices. Rhubarb Rhubarb reviews the previous week and The Crumble serves up crunchy quotes and other memorable moments. The name comes from UK rhyming slang: custard and jelly, telly (TV).

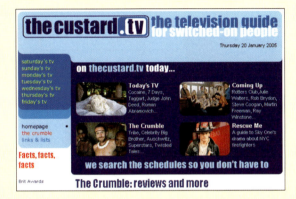

DigiGuide

http://www.digiguide.com/

DigiGuide is a Windows application that enables you to download program information and create customized listings for the United States or the UK and Ireland. Find out more here.

yourTV

http://www.yourtv.com.au/

Tell this Australian listings site where you are and which subscription services you receive and it'll draw up customized listings for yesterday (so you can see what you missed), today, tomorrow or any day in the next week. You can also create a personal guide and get email alerts when your favorite programs hit the screen.

tvnz.co.nz

http://tvnz.co.nz/

TVNZ's Web site has program details and listings for TV1 and TV2. If you want the other channels, you'll have to click elsewhere. Try the Web sites of rivals TV3 (http://www.tv3.co.nz/) and Prime (http://www.primetv.co.nz/).

MediaCorp TV

http://www.mediacorptv.com/

Singapore's MediaCorp TV is responsible for four television channels: Channel 5, Channel 8, Suria and Central. Its Web site provides daily highlights, biographies of MediaCorp artists and an electronic program guide.

SABC Television

http://www.sabctv.co.za/

SABC's site has listings for SABC 1, 2 and 3, viewable up to seven weeks in advance. Select the individual channels for information about new and popular shows and behind the scenes details.

ER

http://www.ertv.com/

The official site for medical drama *ER* has cast and episode guides, images of the sets, a glossary of those incomprehensible medical terms and a message board where you can chat with other fans.

The West Wing

http://www.westwingtv.com/

Warner Bros promotes *The West Wing* with the usual mixture of cast details, episode guides, clips and background material.

corrie.net

http://www.corrie.net/

Fans of popular UK soap *Coronation Street* have created an unofficial guide to the show. Beginners can start with the New to the Street section, which explains the what, who and where. Elsewhere you'll find weekly updates and character and actor profiles.

Neighbours

http://www.neighbours.com/

The Web site for Australia's most famous soap covers the history of the show and its stars and provides episode and character guides.

Star Trek

http://www.startrek.com/

Rumors that the Internet was created solely for the benefit of *Star Trek* fans have yet to be confirmed, but there's certainly no shortage of *Trek* sites. This is the official one, with information about all the different series and movies, character bios, photos, videos, games, a technology library and a database of foods eaten around the *Star Trek* universe. There's even an Introduction to *Star Trek* for the three people who've never encountered it in any of its myriad forms. It's truly Trekkie in scope.

Theater

Broadway.com

http://www.broadway.com/

Broadway.com has the buzz, the star bios, the interviews, the reviews and the tickets for shows on Broadway and in London. You can also put your own questions to various actors and read the replies, which are published on the site.

Playbill On-line

http://www.playbill.com/

The online edition of *Playbill* magazine gives you plenty to read. It has theater news from around the world, listings for the US and London and lots of features, interviews, columns, celebrity talk and obituaries. If you think you know a lot about theater, try the quizzes.

describe it. Some of the entries have been expanded into articles with links to relevant works.

Whatsonstage.com
http://www.whatsonstage.com/

Whatsonstage.com covers the UK theater scene, including drama, music and dance. It has listings and seating plans, details of opening and closings, and reviews of West End, fringe and regional performances. Other highlights include a 20 Questions section that profiles leading performers. Once you've looked at the list of recommended performances, you can purchase tickets online.

TheatreNet.com
http://www.theatrenet.com/

Also focused on the UK, TheatreNet has a weekly news and gossip column, advice on how to book tickets and where to sit, and a useful collection of theater links.

Art

ArtLex
http://www.artlex.com/

Make sense of arty jargon with ArtLex, an illustrated art dictionary that defines over 3,600 terms used by artists, art historians, critics and other people who not only know what they like, but also know how to

Artonline
http://www.artonline.it/eng/

Italian art site with a History section covering the major artists of the past and a XX Century section for modern works. You can also try your hand at jigsaw puzzles made from works of art or track down the Web sites of the world's major museums and galleries.

Metropolitan Museum of Art
http://www.metmuseum.org/

The highlight of the Met's site is the online collection, which features about 6,500 items from the museum. You get highlights from each department plus all of the European paintings, American paintings and American sculpture. You can browse or search by artist, type of work, country of origin, creation date or keyword. The site also has a timeline of art history and visitor information.

Museum of Modern Art

http://www.moma.org/

New York's Museum of Modern Art (MoMA) also shares its collection online. Selected items from the six departments – architecture and design, drawing, film and media, painting and sculpture, photography and prints and illustrated books – are available for browsing. Most have commentary so you can appreciate their place in the art world.

National Gallery

http://www.nationalgallery.org.uk/

The UK's National Gallery presents 12 of its most famous works online. You can view them all together, or by artist or time period, but after a while you'll get bored. That's when you should click across to the Full Collection Index, where you'll find all the other artworks, sorted by artist, with commentary and good-sized reproductions. The site also has beginner's guides that explain some of the stories and subjects depicted in the paintings.

Tate

http://www.tate.org.uk/

The Tate collects British art from 1500 to the present day and modern art from around the world. Details of all the works in the collection are available online, although not all the entries have pictures. Still, you can find out where your favorite items are displayed and go and see them in the flesh. You can also find out what's on at the various galleries.

Le Louvre

http://www.louvre.fr/

Le Louvre goes one better than its rivals with a virtual tour featuring 360-degree panoramas that let you spin round inside its galleries. The site also features selected works from the museum's collections of antiquities, sculptures, paintings and drawings – including its most famous work, Leonardo da Vinci's Mona Lisa.

Books

BookBrowse

http://www.bookbrowse.com/

The bookworms at BookBrowse find interesting books, track down reviews, organize excerpts and interview the authors. You can search or browse by genre, title or author and add your own comments about books you've already read. There's also lots of material for book groups, including advice on finding or starting a group, tips on moderating meetings and reading guides for over 300 books.

London Review of Books

http://www.lrb.co.uk/

The bimonthly *London Review of Books* carries lengthy and literate book reviews, plus essays and columns. If you're looking for literary love, check out the personal ads from the latest edition.

Book World

http://www.washingtonpost.com/bookworld/

The Washington Post brings you reviews, essays and online discussions. If you want to form your own opinions, try the Chapter One section, which provides excerpts from recently published works.

Independent Enjoyment

http://enjoyment.independent.co.uk/books/

The Independent newspaper's Enjoyment section has a user-friendly Books subdivision with literary news, features, interviews and plenty of reviews. Simply run your eye over the list of titles until something takes your fancy.

Project Gutenberg

http://www.gutenberg.org/

Project Gutenberg produces electronic versions of out-of-copyright works and makes them available online. If you're looking for classics, you'll find several thousand of them here.

Humor

Comedy Central

http://www.comedycentral.com/

Comedy Central is best known for *South Park*, but it also broadcasts other shows and stand-up. Find out more here, then waste time with the jokes, games and toys in the Time Wasters section.

The Onion

http://www.theonion.com/

"America's Finest News Source™" satirizes current events. It looks like a newspaper, right down to the datelines and informative graphics, but the stories are… different. Read and enjoy.

Private Eye

http://www.private-eye.co.uk/

The online edition of the UK's *Private Eye* replaces the cheap newsprint of the original with tidy Web pages that don't crease or smudge. It offers a selection of jokes, columns and cartoons from the current issue, plus a very small selection of older material.

Comics.com

http://www.comics.com/

Comics.com features over 90 comic strips and editorial cartoons. It has current and recent strips, desktop diversions such as icons and cursors, and assorted other entertainments.

Jokes.com

http://www.jokes.com/

Thousands of jokes, of variable tastefulness and rated for explicitness. Browse them by category – blonde jokes, lawyer jokes and so on – or simply click the Random Joke button for unspecified laughs.

Random Joke Server

http://www.randomjoke.com/

Select your favorite type of joke for a random offering. The Joke Server offers classic one-liners and light bulb jokes as well as jokes for nerds.

Recreation

You know you ought to spend more time doing things and less time in front of the computer… but let's be honest, sometimes it rains and you don't want to go out. And even your indoor projects require some research. The Internet has plenty of sites about sports and pastimes. You can immerse yourself in facts, theories, statistics and plans… and then get more out of your offline activities.

Food

Epicurious

http://eat.epicurious.com/

Eat, drink and learn at Epicurious. There's a champagne primer and a wine guide, a food dictionary and a set of videos demonstrating everything from the frying of eggs to the zesting of lemons. The star attraction, though, is the recipe collection: over 17,000 of them, browsable by category or searchable by all manner of criteria.

StarChefs

http://starchefs.com/

At StarChefs the cooks are as much of an attraction as the food. Pick a chef, check their bio, read their tips, find out where they work and then – if you like what you've seen so far – try their recipes. It features both restaurant chefs and cookbook authors.

Delia Online

http://www.deliaonline.com/

England's egg queen has a cool and collected site with three main sections: Recipes, Ingredients and Cookery School. The last has illustrated guides to cookery techniques, including instructions for boiling eggs. Once you've got the dinner out of the way, you can read Delia's diary or visit her store.

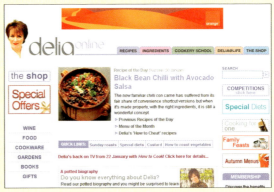

BBC Food

http://www.bbc.co.uk/food/

The BBC does food as well and as thoroughly as it does everything else. Here you'll find biographies of its chefs and presenters, Web pages for all its food programs and a searchable database of recipes. It's left to you to decide whether Rick Stein's Thai Fish Cakes with Green Beans will go with Jamie Oliver's Easiest Sexiest Salad in the World.

All Recipes

http://www.allrecipes.com/

Recipes, recipes and more recipes, by course, ingredient or occasion. If you're overwhelmed by the choice, try the Top Ten section of the Recipe

Index – it lists the best recipes from each of the collections. There's also a Cooking Basics section that tells you what to make and how to make it.

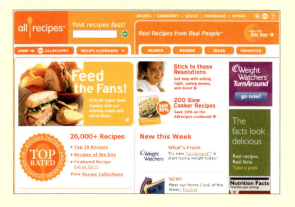

Webicurean

http://www.webicurean.com/

Webicurean makes the most of the Net by linking its articles to material on other sites. It also has forums where you can add comments and recipes.

Messy Gourmet

http://www.messygourmet.com/

Cack-handed and experimental cooks will like Messy Gourmet, a site that proclaims that "cooking is an experience to be savored by all senses... the steam, the aromas, the colors... the mess". Only the articles from the current issue are immediately obvious – check the archives for more.

KidChef

http://www.kidchef.com/

KidChef serves up advice and recipes for younger chefs. The Before You Start section emphasizes safety and clearing up afterwards, and the Cooktionary explains all the terms. From there you can proceed to the recipes, which are categorized by type and skill level.

Accidental Scientist

http://www.exploratorium.edu/cooking/

You aren't just making a meal, you're engaged in practical chemistry. The Cooking section of The Accidental Scientist explains the science behind your culinary endeavors. Find out what happens when you bake bread, make a naked egg (!) and learn how smell affects flavor.

Cook's Thesaurus

http://www.foodsubs.com/

You've got all the ingredients except one – and it's something you've never heard of. Can you use something else instead? The Cook's Thesaurus tells you (and shows you) what things are, then recommends alternatives.

section on the houses featured in the television series. You'll find virtual tours, floor plans, time-lapse movies and Webcams.

iVillage Home & Garden Channel

http://www.ivillage.com/home/

The Home & Garden section of this US megasite covers architecture, home improvement, decorating, crafts and even cleaning and organizing. Find out how to place your furniture, choose the right colors for your walls or find the solutions to four big clutter dilemmas. Sources include *House Beautiful*, *Country Living* and *Good Housekeeping*.

Channel4.com 4homes

http://www.channel4.com/4homes/

Channel 4's 4homes site explains how to buy, sell and renovate houses in the UK. Learn how to make your home attractive to potential buyers, then read about the area you plan to relocate to. You can also find out how to volunteer for television programs on all these subjects.

This Old House Online

http://www.thisoldhouse.com/toh/

This Old House Online accompanies the US magazine and television series of the same name. It has articles and project guides for doer-uppers, plus useful extras such as materials calculators and discussion forums. For inspiration, look at the

BBC Homes

http://www.bbc.co.uk/homes/

The Homes section of the BBC's Web site has all sorts of house-buying and homemaking advice. Click through to the TV and Radio section to follow up on the programs you've seen and find out about the presenters. There's also a DIY section with step-by-step guides, advice on safety and a paint calculator that tells you how many pots you need.

HomePro.com

http://www.homepro.com/

Find a plumber, painter, paver, pool installer or other tradesperson in the UK, then use the jargon buster to work out what they're talking about.

There's also a style magazine with products and projects for everything from the loft to the patio.

Better Homes and Gardens Australia

http://www.bhg.com.au/

The Web site of Australia's *Better Homes and Gardens* magazine has sections for gardening, food, home improvement, craft and better living. Special features include encyclopedias on everything from food and drink to plants, pests and diseases, and DIY. It also has measurement and loan calculators.

Style New Zealand

http://www.nze.co.nz/

Feather your nest with decorating ideas and links to companies that provide products for kitchens, bathrooms, interior and exterior decoration, and outdoor living.

GardenWeb

http://www.gardenweb.com/

The GardenWeb site has lots of resources for gardeners, including a plant database and a botanical glossary, plus over 90 forums covering everything from antique roses and butterfly gardens to tractors and woodlands. Localized versions of the site cater for European and Australasian gardeners.

Garden Advice

http://www.gardenadvice.co.uk/

Find out how to create or renovate a lawn, build and maintain a water garden, or get the best out of your house plants. There's also a special section for kids with projects such as seed collecting and hairy monster pots.

Carry on Gardening

http://www.carryongardening.org.uk/

Carry on Gardening encourages you to keep exercising your green fingers despite accidents, illnesses, disabilities and plain old ageing. It has advice on making your garden accessible plus lots of projects to consider. There's also a Tools section that explains how to use and adapt regular garden implements and reviews specialized tools.

The National Gardens Scheme

http://www.ngs.org.uk/

Find a garden to visit with the NGS's online database of UK properties that are open to the public. You can select your county or search by name, opening dates or specific features.

NZ Gardens Online

http://gardens.co.nz/

Find a garden to visit in New Zealand or peruse the articles and advice. There are special sections for roses and native plants and it has links to other Web sites about gardening in New Zealand.

Care for Animals

http://www.avma.org/careforanimals/

The American Veterinary Medical Association has put together an animated site that provides basic advice on selecting and caring for pets. The Kids section has worksheets to print out and complete.

InfoPet

http://www.infopet.co.uk/

The UK-based InfoPet site provides general information and advice about common and uncommon pets, including cats, dogs, chinchillas, hedgehogs and snakes. It also compiles news and research from various sources and has book reviews and a list of useful contacts.

RSPCA

http://www.rspca.org.uk/

Information about the RSPCA's campaigns, pet-care advice and a Tricky Problems FAQ that explains what to do if you find your cat stuck up a tree.

Battersea Dogs' Home

http://www.dogshome.org/

Find out about the four Rs – rescue, reunite, rehabilitate and rehome – and get advice about finding your lost pet or adopting a stray.

The Dog Hause

http://www.doghause.com/

The Dog Hause is a fun site for pet owners. You won't find much advice here, but it has lots of animal quotes and proverbs, fun facts, clip-art, fonts and sounds. It also has a Spay and Neuter section that encourages pet owners to avoid unwanted litters.

Hobbies

The Genealogy Home Page

http://www.genhomepage.com/

Well-organized collection of links to online genealogy resources. The What's Really New section is updated daily.

RootsWeb.com

http://www.rootsweb.com/

Genealogy site that enables you to get in touch with other genealogists and share your findings. It's sponsored by Ancestry.com, a subscription-based reference site. It also has a guide to tracing your family tree, with links to online resources.

FamilySearch

http://www.familysearch.org/

The FamilySearch site provides online access to genealogical information compiled by The Church of Jesus Christ of Latter-day Saints. Resources include records from the 1880 United States, 1881 British Isles and 1881 Canadian censuses.

Linns.com

http://www.linns.com/

Linns.com is the Web site of the weekly stamp-collecting magazine. It has stamp news, how-to information for beginners and a collection of reference material, including a glossary of philatelic terms. The related Stampsites.com (http://www.stampsites.com/) enables you to search over 15,000 Web pages dealing with stamps.

CoinSite

http://www.coinsite.com/

If you don't fancy stamps, how about coins? CoinSite has a numismatic FAQ covering coins and paper money, reference material, a list of recommended books and an Ask the Coin Doc section that lets you put any remaining questions to the resident expert.

Smithsonian Kids: Collecting

http://kids.si.edu/collecting/

The Collecting section of the Smithsonian's Kids site introduces youngsters to the art of accumulating miscellaneous objects. It explains why people collect things and how to start a collection, then provides information about some of the Smithsonian's collections. It also has video clips in which young collectors show off their booty.

craftster.org

http://www.craftster.org/

Crafts for the Internet generation. With a tag line of "No tea cozies without irony", craftster.org provides discussion forums for people who like to make things… hip, modern things. It covers the entire crafts spectrum, with areas for everything from homewares and clothing to "crafting for good not evil". Just don't mention that tea cozy you're knitting.

Classic Stitches

http://www.classicstitches.com/

Classic Stitches magazine has lots of free charts on its Web site, in PDF format. Some are only available to members of the Classic Stitches Club, but it's free to join. There's also a Know How section with guides to needlecraft techniques and a message board where you can discuss your projects.

World Wide Quilting Page

http://www.quilt.com/

Useful rather than attractive, the World Wide Quilting page has how-to articles, directions and diagrams for lots of traditional quilt blocks, a message board and links to other quilting sites.

The Quilt Index

http://www.quiltindex.org/

Find inspiration with The Quilt Index, an online catalogue featuring images of hundreds of American quilts. You can view the quilts by time period, style, purpose or region.

Pottery Making Illustrated

http://www.potterymaking.org/

The highlight of *Pottery Making Illustrated's* Web site is the Techniques section, which has step-by-step slideshows covering various tasks. There's also a collection of glaze recipes and a small selection of articles from the current issue.

Woodworker's Central

http://www.woodworking.org/

Get chopping, sawing, carving and turning with Woodworker's Central, a vast resource with links to articles and plans from around the Web. It also has tool reviews, book reviews, a sampler with photos of different woods and a message board. If you think you know a lot about wood, try to navigate through the maze by answering questions about it.

art-e-zine

http://www.art-e-zine.co.uk/

UK site "for everyone that's interested in playing and having fun with paper, paints, inks and stamps, and any other exciting mediums". Here you'll find tag art (creative luggage labels), collages, art journals, a paper doll gallery and other papery concoctions.

Oriland

http://www.oriland.com/

Novel origami site that displays folded characters and structures in virtual worlds. Instructions for some of the models are available in the Origami Studio. The Oriland University has an overview of origami, a guide to the symbols and a set of lessons.

Alex's Paper Planes

http://www.paperairplanes.co.uk/

Build yourself a fleet of aeroplanes with the diagrams and instructions on this site. Projects are classified as easy, medium or hard to make and come with flying instructions. You'll also find a helicopter, a blimp, a rocket and a paper frisbee.

photo.net

http://www.photo.net/

Vast photography Web site with lots of great images to inspire you. It has equipment reviews, advice, busy forums and a gallery where you can upload your photos and have them criticized. There's also a Travel section with illustrated travelogues.

Digital Photography Review

http://www.dpreview.com/

If you're looking for a digital camera, Digital Photography Review has all the latest news plus in-depth reviews of most of the cameras on the market. Other features include an imaging glossary and forums where you can find out what other Internet users think about particular cameras.

ShortCourses

http://www.shortcourses.com/

Find out how to choose and use a digital camera with this collection of electronic books. In spite of the "ShortCourses" moniker, the guides are comprehensive and clearly written. It also has printable pocket guides for popular cameras.

Automotive

Motor Trend Online

http://www.motortrend.com/

US site with industry news, road tests and features from *Motor Trend* magazine. Check out the Future Vehicles section for predictions for the next few years, concept cars and sneak previews of forthcoming models. You can also read about the car, truck and sport/utility vehicle of the year.

Car and Driver

http://www.caranddriver.com/

Car and Driver's Web site has buyer's guides for new and used cars, reviews, comparison tests and user's road tests. There's also a report on the supercar challenge to find "the baddest in all the land" and a 10 Best Cars section with cars from the last 20 years.

Top Gear

http://www.topgear.com/

The site of the UK television program and magazine has lots of everything: news, features, opinion columns, reviews, advice on buying and owning a car, valuations and readers' letters. The inimitable

Jeremy Clarkson appears at the top but doesn't (at the time of writing) have much to say.

CarTalk

http://www.cartalk.com/

CarTalk is a US radio show featuring mechanics Tom and Ray Magliozzi. Listen to the latest broadcast online or read all sorts of entertaining articles and columns. There's a lot here that's just for fun, such as the electronic traffic tickets you can send to your friends, but there's also plenty of useful advice.

Road & Travel

http://www.roadandtravel.com/

Although it isn't immediately obvious, Road and Travel is aimed primarily at women who want to go places, by car or otherwise. It has buying guides, reviews, maintenance tips, safety and security advice and road humor – minus the endless cracks about women drivers, obviously.

MINI.com

http://www.mini.com/

Find out about the funky new Mini from this stylish site. It has games, video clips and interactive features as well as the lowdown on the car. Localized versions are available for many countries.

Harley-Davidson.com

http://www.harley-davidson.com/

Feel the wind in your hair at the Harley-Davidson site, which has riding and maintenance advice as well as details of the bikes. You can also find out about renting a Harley or going on an official tour.

The Antique Motorbike Club of America

http://www.antiquemotorcycle.org/

The main attraction on the Antique Motorbike Club's site is the virtual tour of its museum. Panoramic images give you a 360-degree view of the interior. Click through to the Extended Museum for more details and rotating images of 36 bikes.

MCN

http://www.motorcyclenews.com/

UK motorcycling magazine *MCN* has a busy Web site with classified ads, news, bike and product reviews and a dealer locator. Sport has its own section, with subsections for WSB, British, off-road and MotoGP.

Bikersweb

http://www.bikersweb.co.uk/

Bikersweb is an independent online magazine covering the UK bike scene. It has news, show reports, forums and reader's photographs.

Sport

football365.com

http://www.football365.com/

This British football (soccer) site is updated 365 days a year – hence the title. It offers a daily newspaper delivered by email plus lots of news, views, humor and games. Where else are you going to find an article on the drinking habits of football managers, a list of the top ten mixed metaphors or a collection of famous footballers and their lookalikes? Beyond that it does, of course, have all the results and statistics your football-loving heart desires.

Soccernet

http://soccernet.espn.go.com/

Long-standing soccer site that's now part of ESPN. It covers the English and Scottish Premier Leagues, Europe, the Champions League and global soccer.

Extras include a fantasy league and reports from fans of the English Premiership teams.

FIFA

http://www.fifa.com/

The official site of the official body (the Fédération Internationale de Football Association, to give it its full name) has round-ups of recent events, lots of fact sheets, regulations and the rules of the game.

UEFA

http://www.uefa.com/

UEFA's site has the lowdown on the Champions League, with audio and video to liven things up. It's also developing a Training Ground section with information on playing, coaching and refereeing and there's a Fanzone with games and forums.

Planet Rugby

http://www.planet-rugby.com/

Planet Rugby has lots of news that can be viewed on the main page or sorted by country. It also has opinion columns, a regular discussion of rules and refs, a rugby lookalikes feature that matches up players and celebrities, and some fun and games.

Scrum.com

http://www.scrum.com/

Scrum.com gives you more news, by country or tournament, plus features, columns, a fitness section, a primer for beginners and a rugby dictionary. There's even a section for women's rugby.

World of Rugby League

http://www.rleague.com/

The other sort of rugby also has a Web site, with all the usual news, results and stats, plus coverage of the World Sevens. Australia, New Zealand and Great Britain dominate the coverage, but it also has links to rugby league sites in countries as diverse as the United States, Russia and Fiji.

NFL.com

http://www.nfl.com/

Find out what's happening in the American football world with the official site for the NFL. It has scores, stats, schedules and standings, plus many other things not beginning with "s". There's news, of course, plus radio broadcasts that you can listen to over the Internet, depth charts and links to the official sites of all the teams. If you have a broadband connection, don't miss the NFL Films TV section.

Play Football

http://www.playfootball.com/

Play Football is the NFL's site for kids and thus has brighter colors, shorter words and fewer numbers. It explains the positions, the equipment and the field, tells kids what it's like to be a player and posts the latest scores. Kids can also play football-related games or get off the couch and get involved.

AFL

http://afl.com.au/

Follow football with an Aussie accent at the official site of the Australian Football League. It has audio and video coverage as well as news, results and details of all the clubs and players. There's also a Laws section and a collection of info sheets. Fun features include games, screensavers and wallpaper.

NBA.com

http://www.nba.com/

The National Basketball Association gets covered with typical American thoroughness on NBA.com. Here you'll find news, previews, reviews, player files and more statistics than Michael Jordan could dunk. And when you get tired of reading, you can

look at the photographs and watch the videos. A companion site covers the WNBA.

Inside Hoops

http://www.insidehoops.com/

Inside Hoops covers the entire (American) basketball spectrum, from the pro leagues to college and high school basketball to streetball. Highlights include a rumors page and a daily recap.

SLAM Online

http://www.slamonline.com/

Online edition of the basketball magazine with attitude. Read the features, grab some cool desktop wallpaper and crash the (message) boards to chat with other bball fans.

NHL.com

http://www.nhl.com/

Another game, another fine collection of news, scores, schedules and stats. This time it's ice hockey, with live audio from the games and video highlights for those who're prepared to pay. It also has a rulebook, features on the history of the game and a special section on the Stanley Cup.

SLAM! Sports: Hockey

http://slam.canoe.ca/Slam/Hockey/

The Hockey section of SLAM! Sports provides a Canadian perspective on ice hockey. Select your favorite team for news and results or read the commentary in the Puckmaster column.

CricInfo

http://www.cricinfo.com/

It's just cricket at CricInfo, the stat-happy home of the game that takes breaks for afternoon tea. Features include live ball-by-ball score cards for selected matches, stats, player files, more stats, a database of grounds, a StatGuru, ratings, photographs and forums where you can talk about… stats, of course.

Cricket365

http://www.cricket365.com/

Cricket news and views, 365 days a year… except when rain stops play. Even then it has plenty of fun

features to keep you entertained, including a lookalikes feature and a Mouthing Off column with quotes such as, "There's Neil Harvey standing at leg slip with his legs wide apart waiting for a tickle."

Major League Baseball

http://mlb.mlb.com/

The MLB site is eerily similar to the NFL and NHL sites – and not just because of its penchant for initials. Once again, there's audio and video (and as with the NHL site, you have to take out a subscription for full access).

Baseball

http://www.usatoday.com/sports/baseball/front.htm

USA Today's baseball site has scores and stats, ratings by Jeff Sagarin, team notebooks and a week-by-week archive that lets you click back in time.

The Tennis Server

http://www.tennisserver.com/

Long-standing tennis site with links to news stories from around the Web and an interesting set of columns covering everything from the state of the game to the science of tennis to advice for amateurs. How can you pass up a column called Mortal Tennis that "brings you insight into the trials and tribulations of the everyday player"?

Wimbledon

http://www.wimbledon.com/

The most famous of the Grand Slam tournaments gets the cyber treatment and comes up green and purple. Highlights include a virtual tour with panoramic images, stills and Webcams. There's also a Video Vault with clips from classic matches. The store ships official merchandise around the world, so you can fill your bathroom with green and purple Wimbledon towels.

Davis Cup

http://www.daviscup.com/

Find out which countries are still in the Davis Cup with the official site, which has details of the history and structure of the competition, a list of champions going back to 1900, drawsheets, updates and results.

PGA.com

http://www.pga.com/

Spoil a good walk at the official site of the Professional Golfers' Association of America. It has event and tour schedules with links to the relevant Web sites, a Lesson Book covering everything from swing fundamentals to the mental side of the game, instructional videos and a section for juniors.

Golf Today

http://www.golftoday.co.uk/

Golf Today has news and tour coverage, course directories for the UK and Ireland (plus limited coverage of the rest of the world) and a set of online tutorials. There's also a virtual golf club offering various discounts and other benefits for members.

Olympics

http://www.olympic.org/

The official site of the Olympic movement profiles over 300 Olympic heroes from the summer and winter games. Each athlete gets a write-up and photo gallery and there are videos of some performances. It also has a Sports section with details of all the disciplines that are (or were) included and an Olympic Games section with accounts of all the games since 1896.

IAAF.org

http://www.iaaf.org/

The Web site of the International Association of Athletics Federations brings you track and field news, results, records and rankings. The most interesting feature is the athletes' journals.

Track and Field News.com

http://www.trackandfieldnews.com/

Don't come here for news, although it does link you to results from recent events, but for stats. The Lists section details the top performances from the current year. The Rankings section gives you the top ten performers for each event for every year from 1947 onwards. The Records section has the world records.

Cyclingnews.com

http://www.cyclingnews.com/

The "world center of cycling" has an immensely busy front page linking you to dozens of features and reports. A random sampling of items includes a review of energy bars, an interview with Stuart O'Grady, an article about altitude training, a feature on a female soigneur and results from races in Australia, Belgium, France, Spain and the USA.

Tour de France

http://www.letour.fr/

The official site for cycling's most famous event has details of the next race and results from the most recent one. Highlights include an animated map.

SquashTalk.com

http://www.squashtalk.com/

Independent squash site covering events from around the world. It has several regular columns, a Player of the Month and a Hall of Fame section.

MegaSpin

http://www.megaspin.net/

MegaSpin covers table tennis, otherwise known as ping-pong, "the game that is usually played in the basement with an opponent, with plastic paddles in hand that [make] the distinctive noises when a ball [is] struck." This site covers everything from the equipment required for the basic basement game to the results from international events.

International Gymnast

http://www.intlgymnast.com/

Somersault to the Web site of *International Gymnast* magazine for a frequently updated news page and live reports from major events. It covers both artistic and rhythmic gymnastics.

Gymn

http://www.gymn-forum.com/

Gymn has brief biographies of gymnasts, a gymnastics FAQ, a calendar of upcoming events and lots of links to other gymnastics resources.

SkateWeb: The Figure Skating Page

http://www.frogsonice.com/skateweb/

SkateWeb catalogs figure skating Web pages. The front page highlights recent and upcoming events, making it easy to find coverage of competitions. New sites also enjoy a brief spell on a front page before being moved into the appropriate category: Reference, News & Features, Elite Skaters and so on. Brief descriptions are provided where necessary.

Transworld Skateboarding

http://www.skateboarding.com/skate/

Enter the world of ollies and salad grinds with Transworld Skateboarding. It has photos and a few videos, trick tips, message boards and a buyer's guide that tells you what the pros are riding.

NASCAR.COM

http://www.nascar.com/

The Nascar site has news, results, driver profiles and a wealth of background information. The subscription-based TrackPass section provides live coverage and on-demand multimedia.

Formula1.com

http://www.formula1.com/

The official Formula 1 site has lots of news, pages for all the teams with car specs and driver bios, attractive circuit maps and live coverage of races.

ITV f1

http://www.itv-f1.com/

ITV's Formula 1 coverage merits a special section of the ITV site, with news, photo features, pictures of pit babes and paddock boys, humorous digging by The Mole and a driver diary. You can also find out what the commentary team has been up to.

Outdoors

GORP

http://gorp.away.com/

The Great Outdoor Recreation Pages should be the first place you visit when you get the urge for fresh air. It's huge, energetic and most of all enthusiastic, with lots of get-out-and-do-it guides to places, activities – from biking and camping to snorkeling and skiing – and the necessary equipment.

Outside Online

http://outsidemag.com/

Another great site, this is the online edition of *Outside* magazine. It has four main sections: Gear, Travel, Bodywork (getting fit) and Archives. The last has articles from previous issues of the magazine – such as "I Will Survive", ten on-the-edge accounts of getting caught in an avalanche, knocked down by a volcano or chewed by a grizzly bear.

Backpacker.com

http://www.backpacker.com/

Read the reviews to choose the best boots, rucksacks and other equipment, then go hiking in the US and Canada. It also has a Technique section covering health, nutrition and nature. Want to know how to prevent blisters or make gourmet meals in the wilderness? The answers are here.

Outdoor Britain

http://www.visitbritain.com/uk/
outdoorbritain/

Outdoor Britain encourages you to "experience the beauty of Britain's countryside by snorkeling through a bog or chasing cheese down a hill". Or if those very British activities don't take your fancy, you can take inspiration from authors, composers, artists, films and myths that have described or depicted the countryside. Once you're ready to leave your desk, the site recommends locations for walking, cycling, horse riding, fishing, water activities and extreme sports.

Geocaching

http://www.geocaching.com/

Discover geocaching, a new sport where you use your GPS unit to track down a cache – a hiding place where items can be concealed. You can then make an entry in the logbook, take something from the cache, leave something for the next person to find and go on your way. It's a high-tech treasure hunt.

mtbREVIEW.com

http://www.mtbr.com/

Forsake the highways at mtbREVIEW.com. It has a product database with reviews by riders, details of over 6,000 trails around the US and Tech Talk message boards covering everything from wheels and brakes to riding and training techniques.

Mountain Biking UK

http://www.mbuk.com/

The Web site of the popular UK mountain biking magazine has bike and kit tests, a Grime Time area with step-by-step instructions for setting up, maintaining and mending your bike, riding masterclasses and racing news.

Birding on the Web

http://www.birder.com/

Extensive resource for birdwatchers, with lists of birding hotspots, advice for backyard birders and links to lots of other birding sites.

BirdSource

http://www.birdsource.org/

Interesting site that enables US birders to get involved in research projects by recording and sharing their observations. The instructions and results – especially for the FeederWatch project – are worth reading even if you're based elsewhere.

Outdoor Life

http://www.outdoorlife.com/outdoor/

The online edition of US hunting and fishing magazine *Outdoor Life* has lots of advice on catching

your own dinner. The Fish Finder covers over 90 game fish, with techniques and gear tips, and the Game Finder explains how to shoot everything from mourning doves to black bears. The site also has reviews of everything from socks to trucks.

Tales of the Ultimate Sportsmen

http://www.ultimatesportsmen.com/

Lots of stories about the ones that got away – and more to the point, the ones that didn't.

The Daily Sail

http://www.madforsailing.com/

The Daily Sail is a subscription-based site with sailing news and features. Sign up for a free trial and read about offshore, inshore and dinghy racing. If you're feeling mean, go straight to the Disaster pages and read about other people's misfortunes.

The Boating Info Centre

http://www.boating.co.nz/

New Zealand boating site, with the emphasis on sailing. There's advice on preparing for and sailing in races and improving your speed.

DiverNET

http://www.divernet.com/

The UK's *DIVER* magazine republishes most of its features on the Web. Its informative site has articles on training, travel, marine life and photography, gear reviews and a regularly updated News section. It also has forums where you can make contact with other British divers.

Scuba Board

http://www.scubaboard.com/

Popular and busy diving message board covering everything from learning to dive to deeply technical wreck and cave diving. It's a good place to ask questions, get opinions on gear and read about dive destinations around the world.

SKI Magazine

http://www.skimag.com/skimag/

Find the snow with SKI Magazine. Its extensive site has North American and international snow reports, gear reviews and photo essays. If you're struggling to stay on your feet, check out the Instruction section, where you'll find features on fitness, technique and avoiding accidents.

thealps.com

http://www.thealps.com/

Check out the snow at both ends of the world with thealps.com. It covers resorts in Europe, Utah and New Zealand, providing details of the ski areas, facilities, activities and accommodation. It also has weather reports for some resorts.

MountainZone.com

http://www.mountainzone.com/

MountainZone.com takes you to the top of the world, by bike, crampon and karabiner, and then down again on skis or a snowboard. It also covers the newly popular sport of adventure racing. For inspiration, look at the spectacular images in the Photography section.

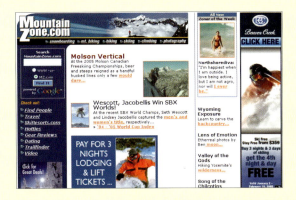

In the real world, you might feel isolated, but on the Internet, there's always someone who shares your concerns. Whether you're looking for help with health problems or want to get in touch with people who are confronting the same issues, there are lots of great resources on the Web.

Health

HealthFinder

http://www.healthfinder.gov/

HealthFinder directs you to online health information. The links were compiled by the US Department of Health and Human Services, so the sites should be reputable – but you should still read critically and exercise your judgement. Resources can be accessed by topic or interest group.

WebMD Health

http://my.webmd.com/

WebMD's Health section has two basic types of material: medical information about diseases and conditions, and health and wellness advice to help you avoid needing the medical stuff. It's aimed at laypeople and the articles are attractively presented and clearly written.

MEDLINEplus

http://medlineplus.gov/

MEDLINEplus features health information from the US National Library of Medicine. Find out about diseases and conditions, look up medicines, explore the medical encyclopedia and check medical terms in the dictionary. If you still aren't satisfied, go to the Other Resources section and follow the links to MEDLINE itself, a searchable database with information about articles published in over 4,000 medical journals.

NHS Direct Online

http://www.nhsdirect.nhs.uk/

The UK's NHS Direct Online is another gateway to health information. It has a health encyclopedia, a self-help guide to help you interpret your own symptoms and a section on healthy living.

Australian Department of Health and Ageing

http://www.health.gov.au/

The Australian Department of Health and Ageing provides an A to Z guide linking you to Web sites on its programs, subjects and initiatives. For general advice, click through to Health Insite (http://www.healthinsite.gov.au/). It has lots of health information accessible by lifestyle, disease or condition, life event and population group.

OncoLink

http://www.oncolink.com/

OncoLink specializes in cancer. Created by experts at the University of Pennsylvania, it has articles about different types of cancers, treatment options and coping strategies. If you need cheering up, try the art gallery, which features work by cancer patients – many of them children.

KidsHealth.org

http://www.kidshealth.org/

KidsHealth has separate areas for parents, children and teenagers. The Kids section is fun and has an interactive tour of the body as well as articles and advice. A glossary defines the big words and explains how to say them. Parents miss out on some of the entertainment, but they do get information about everything from first aid to behavioral problems.

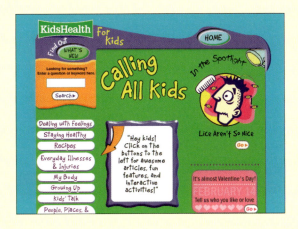

Go Ask Alice!

http://www.goaskalice.columbia.edu/

Go Ask Alice! is a medical question-and-answer site run by Columbia University. School and university students (and anyone else) can ask questions anonymously and read the replies on the site. Since Alice has been answering questions for a long time, there's a good chance your question has already been asked – in which case you can find the answer by browsing or searching.

Men's Health

http://www.menshealth.com/

The Web site of *Men's Health* magazine has "tons of useful stuff" about fitness, weight loss, health and sex. Find out how to shed that stomach and get a cover-model body while avoiding a heart attack and giving your girlfriend a night to remember.

iVillage Health

http://www.ivillagehealth.com/

The Health section of iVillage covers issues for women and families. Browse the site by topic or put your questions to the panel of experts, specialists in everything from eye health to emotional well-being.

Disabilities

Disability Now

http://www.disabilitynow.org.uk/

The Web site of UK campaigning newspaper *Disability Now* has news and features from the latest issue plus an archive of older material. Each of the current campaigns has its own section.

Youreable.com

http://www.youreable.com/

Youreable was created as the result of a television competition to win business support for a new Internet venture. The nicely designed site provides information for disabled people, including headline news, plus details of products and services. It also has forums where you can discuss subjects such as benefits, equipment, motoring and work.

RNIB

http://www.rnib.org.uk/

The UK's Royal National Institute for the Blind uses its Web site to provide the answers to questions such as, "What can blind and partially sighted people see?" and, "Who can register as blind?" It also has lots of information about designing accessible Web sites and a (small) directory of sites that have been awarded the RNIB's See it Right logo.

Sign Community

http://www.signcommunity.org.uk/

The British Deaf Association's Sign Community Web site campaigns for recognition of British Sign Language (BSL). There's also a directory of over 1,700 relevant groups, organizations and services across the UK.

EnableNet

http://www.enable.net.au/

Australia's EnableNet aims to be a resource on disabilities and a meeting place for people who are affected by them. Currently it has news headlines, a chat area and message boards. There's a directory of Web sites and books that provide further information and it catalogs online services that make life easier for people with disabilities.

EnableNZ

http://www.enable.co.nz/

Enable NZ assists people who are affected by disabilities. Its Web site has a range of resources, including information about funding, a searchable equipment database, an catalog detailing items in its library (which can be requested online) and a directory of relevant Web sites.

Family

Yahooligans!

http://www.yahooligans.com/

Yahooligans! is a version of the Web directory designed for young browsers. It works just like the grown-up version, but concentrates on sites for kids. Special features include Ask Earl, a weekday column in which cartoon characters Earl and Stray Kat use the Web to answer questions submitted by children. There's also a section for parents with information about safe surfing.

Nickelodean Online

http://www.nick.com/

The Web site of the popular children's television channel is all about fun, games, cartoons and interactivity. Kids can select their favorite show for character files, clips, message boards and lots of games, or simply click around the sections and see what they find. It'll keep them happily occupied for hours on end.

National Geographic Homework Help

http://www.nationalgeographic.com/education/homework/

National Geographic's homework site brings together all the fact-filled features that'll be useful for projects and reports. If there's an assignment on animals, science, history or, of course, geography, you'll find material here. Once the homework is done, there are games and activities in the Kids site.

SOFWeb

http://www.sofweb.vic.edu.au/

SOFWeb is a reference site with resources of its own and links to the best education sites around the

Web. It's run by the Department of Education and Training in Victoria, Australia, but students and teachers from other countries will also find it useful.

Oxfam's CoolPlanet

http://www.oxfam.org.uk/coolplanet/

Oxfam's CoolPlanet informs teachers and children about global issues such as poverty and fair trade. Kids can check out the World section for information about some of the countries where the charity works, then visit the Take Action section for things to do, both in the real world and online.

Raising Kids

http://www.raisingkids.co.uk/

Find out what to do with your kids (no, you can't just leave them on the bus) with Raising Kids, a UK site that covers youngsters of all ages and stages. Learn what to expect from your baby, how to toilet train your toddler or encourage your child to eat properly at school, and get advice on the troublesome teenage years. There are lots of articles here, and if you don't find what you're looking for, you can put your questions to an expert.

Mumsnet

http://www.mumsnet.com/

The UK-based Mumsnet enables mothers – and fathers – to share their experiences. Find the best childcare products (and submit your own opinions),

get advice from childcare experts, find out how to teach your child to count, read or swim, and talk to other parents via the message boards.

Mumsweb

http://www.mumsweb.com.au/

Australia's Mumsweb is a community site that enables parents to discuss everything from pregnancy to helping kids through a divorce. Add your comments to the articles, contribute a feature of your own or join other parents in the chat rooms.

Older people

American Association of Retired People

http://www.aarp.org/

AARP's Web site covers everything from money and work to travel and leisure. There's loads of information on all the issues affecting older people, plus a great Learning and Technology section with reviews and "how-to" guides.

ThirdAge

http://www.thirdage.com/

ThirdAge caters to people who aren't quite seniors: "first-wave baby boomers, adults in their mid-40s through 50s". If your kids have moved out – or are about to – and you have more free time, visit this site for beauty and style advice, a tech section for people who weren't born with joysticks in their hands, a genealogy section and articles on health, love, money and travel.

Over50s.com

http://www.over50s.com/

Over50s.com is a UK-based site with news, features on finance and health, and a legal section dealing with issues such as divorce and will-making. It also covers subjects such as travel, careers, motoring and relationships.

SAGA

http://www.saga.co.uk/

The Saga Group is best known for organizing holidays for British over-50s. A visit to its Web site reveals a multitude of other activities, from health and financial services to radio stations (you can listen online), a magazine and Circles, a service for finding old friends and making new ones.

Alzheimer's Association

http://www.alz.org/

The Alzheimer's Association site has information about the condition, updates on the latest research, message boards, poems and short stories, and a "Maintain Your Brain" section that helps you keep your grey matter in good shape. There's something for everyone, whether you're suffering from memory loss, a caregiver or a medical professional.

Sexuality

PlanetOut

http://www.planetout.com/

PlanetOut is a US portal for lesbians, bisexuals and gay men. It has articles on money and careers, family issues, health and fitness and romance, plus coverage of Pride events around the world and a busy personals section.

Gay.com

http://www.gay.com/

In addition to the global site, Gay.com has offshoots for various countries, including the UK and Australia. It has political, financial and entertainment news, features on lifestyle, health and HIV, and a travel section. Members also get access to chat rooms, personals, email and message boards.

RainbowNetwork.com

http://www.rainbownetwork.com/

RainbowNetwork is a UK site for lesbians and gay men, with news, shopping and travel sections, members-only areas for men and women, forums and personal ads. There are lots of fun features as well, including top-ten lists, games, quizzes and tips on everything from surviving the Christmas party to becoming a porn star.

glbtq

http://www.glbtq.com/

glbtq is an encyclopedia of gay, lesbian, transgender and queer culture. Serious and somewhat academic, it has more than 1,200 entries in three categories: Arts, Literature and Social Sciences.

New Mardi Gras

http://www.mardigras.org.au/

Online home of Sydney's world-famous gay and lesbian Mardi Gras. Look at photos from previous years, find out what's happening at the next parade, volunteer your services or make a donation.

Religion

ReligiousResources.org

http://www.religiousresources.org/

Extensive and well-organized database of religious (mostly Christian) resources. Find religious texts, theology sites and religious organizations, electronic communities, clip-art, music and much more.

BuddhaNet

http://www.buddhanet.net/

BuddhaNet provides information and educational resources for people from all Buddhist traditions. Features include a basic Buddhism guide, a library of electronic books and a Web directory.

The Hindu Universe

http://www.hindunet.org/

The Hindu Universe is a resource center with news, horoscopes, an event calendar, lots of educational materials and a Web directory. Find out about Hindu philosophy and customs, read about Ayurveda and yoga or chat in the forums.

Al-Islam

http://www.al-islam.com/

The multilingual Al-Islam has information from the Qur'an and Hadith, an Islamic dictionary, prayer-time and Zakah calculators, and a guide to Hajj and 'Umrah. There's also a Discover Islam section that introduces the concepts and principles.

Godulike

http://www.godulike.co.uk/

Irreverent site that provides an unbeliever's overview of more than 100 faiths. Find out what people believe and which gods they worship, then review the Godulike scorecard. Religions are rated on such qualities as "belief in any sort of existence after death", "clear and understandable explanations" and "chance of world domination". Whether it amuses, intrigues or offends depends on your point of view.

Shopping and Services

Internet shopping has exploded over the last few years, thanks to the development of encryption technologies that protect your credit-card details as they travel across the Internet. You can buy all sorts of things, from books and CDs to computers and cars – but do check that the store can deliver to your area. You can also use the Internet for banking, job hunting and travel.

Guides

Shopping.com

http://www.shopping.com/

Shopping.com unites two popular shopping services: DealTime, a price-comparison tool, and Epinions, a collector of consumer reviews. The new site, available in both US and UK versions, enables you to search for products, compare prices and opinions, and then click through to an online merchant.

ShoppingSpot

http://www.shoppingspot.com/

ShoppingSpot is a US-based site that links you to price-comparison tools, advice and product reviews as well as online stores. It only lists major retailers, but sometimes that's all you need.

Kelkoo

http://www.kelkoo.com/

Kelkoo is a shopping search engine with branches in ten European countries, including the UK. It helps you find products and compare prices.

2020Shops

http://www.2020shops.com/

2020Shops is a UK guide to online shopping, with a directory of reviewed and rated stores, price comparisons from DealTime and details of bargains and special offers.

GoodShoppingGuide.com.au

http://goodshoppingguide.com.au/

GoodShoppingGuide showcases bargains and offers from selected Australian online stores. The range of stores is quite limited, so you may not find everything you're looking for.

Books

Amazon.com

http://www.amazon.com/

Probably the best-known store on the Internet, the US-based Amazon started out as a bookseller, but now offers all sorts of things, including CDs, DVDs, toys, games, electronics and clothing (international customers can only purchase some of these products, but Amazon has local sites for several countries including Canada and the UK). It's still best known for books and has lots of features that make it easy to pick something off the virtual shelves, including customer reviews and sample pages from some titles.

Barnes & Noble

http://www.bn.com/

If you don't find the book you're looking for at Amazon, try the online home of real-world US bookstore Barnes & Noble. In addition to regular fiction and nonfiction, it has sections for business and technical books, children's books and calendars. You can also look for bargains in the Sale Annex or track down out-of-print books. If you aren't sure what to read next, join one of the online book clubs or sign up for email newsletters and writer alerts.

Bookbrain.co.uk

http://www.bookbrain.co.uk/

BookBrain is a useful tool for UK book buyers. Enter the title, author or ISBN of the book you're looking for and it'll search for it in 14 online stores, then show you who has it and what they're charging. Surprisingly worthwhile, because even paperbacks can vary in price significantly.

bol.com

http://www.uk.bol.com/

BOL sells books in the UK, several European countries and China. The UK branch concentrates on value rather than range and offers significant discounts: at least 60 per cent off best-sellers and at least 20 per cent off everything else. To take advantage of these prices, you have to become a member, which involves making a second purchase within six months of your initial one.

Collins Booksellers

http://www.collinsbooks.com.au/

Collins Booksellers is an Australian chain with real-world and online stores. The Internet branch enables you to browse by department or search by title, description, author or ISBN. There's also a Bargain Books area with discounted titles.

Kalahari.net

http://www.kalahari.net/

South Africa's Kalahari.net sells books, music, videos and DVDs, software and more, in English and Afrikaans. Useful features include a wish list that keeps track of products that you'd like to buy but aren't quite ready to purchase. It delivers internationally as well as within South Africa.

Music and film

CD Universe

http://www.cduniverse.com/

CD Universe sells music, movies and games. You can browse by genre or search for artists, titles, songs, soundtracks or labels. If you still haven't found what you're looking for, check out the top sellers, recent releases, future releases and music charts. It has track listings and sound samples, cross references to other albums and customer reviews.

a&b sound

http://www.absound.ca/

Canada's a&b sound sells music, movies and electronics – chiefly audiovisual gear and telephones. You can search for specific products or browse by category and artist. It has track listings for CDs and you can stream music over the Internet to see if you're buying the right thing.

101cd.com

http://www.101cd.com/

101cd.com is a UK-based music, video and games store that ships internationally. It carries over 1.6 million titles, including over one million imports, plus related merchandise such as t-shirts, patches and calendars.

SecondSpin.com

http://www.secondspin.com/

SecondSpin.com sells (and buys) used CDs, videos and DVDs, enabling you to stretch your budget or pick up hard-to-find titles. It ships internationally and will replace any item that's scratched or faulty. If you need some cash, visit the Sell to Us page to find out how much your old discs are worth.

DVD Empire

http://www.dvdempire.com/

DVD Empire is a US store that ships internationally. For those outside the US, the upside is that films are usually available long before they come out anywhere else. The downside is that the discs are Region 1 and NTSC, so make sure you'll be able to play them before you place your order.

Sendit.com

http://www.sendit.com/

Sendit.com is a UK-based store selling DVDs, videos, games and stuff – MP3 players, phones, remote controls and so on. Special features include an email service that notifies you when current cinema releases make it to video or DVD and a video hunt service for hard-to-find titles. As long as you're happy with a PAL VHS video or a Region 2 DVD, it'll send it internationally.

Take 2

http://www.take2.co.za/

Take 2 sells music, videos, DVDs, games and electronics to customers within South Africa and in neighboring countries. A Best-sellers page provides easy access to the most popular titles in all formats and you can prebook the top future releases.

Netgrocer

http://www.netgrocer.com/

Netgrocer delivers nonperishable groceries and general merchandise throughout the continental US. Food items are sorted into virtual aisles and there's plenty of information about each product.

Tesco

http://www.tesco.com/

In the UK, save yourself a trip to the supermarket with Tesco's home delivery service. Select your groceries from the virtual shelves, then let someone else do your shopping and bring it round.

Woolworths HomeShop

http://www.homeshop.com.au/

Woolworths offers Internet grocery shopping in Sydney, Canberra and Melbourne. You can browse the shelves by category or search for products.

Cold Storage

http://www.coldstorage.com.sg/

Cold Storage's Online service lets you order groceries for delivery throughout Singapore. You need to be familiar with its range to interpret the terse descriptions, though most items have pictures.

TheDrinkShop.com

http://www.thedrinkshop.com/

Drinks are "on the mouse" at TheDrinkShop.com. It stocks beer, wine, spirits and soft drinks and sells single bottles as well as cases. You can even order a bottle opener. It delivers within the UK and to some European countries.

Cellarmasters

http://www.cellarmasters.com.au/

Cellarmasters delivers wine throughout Australia. You can order regular or mixed cases, or subscribe to a wine plan for regular deliveries. There's plenty of information to help you make your decision.

Flowers

1-800-Flowers.com

http://www.1800flowers.com/

1-800-Flowers.com delivers flowers, plants, gourmet treats, sweets and gifts to the US. It can also arrange international delivery of flowers – select the recipient's country to see what's on offer.

Fleurop-Interflora

http://www.interflora.com/

Fleurop-Interflora's Web site lets you select flowers for delivery to any country. The range depends on the destination – for the US it includes bouquets, baskets and the traditional dozen roses. You can also specify a color and let the florist make up a bouquet of seasonal blooms.

0800flowers.com

http://www.0800flowers.com/

0800flowers.com is a virtual florist that delivers to the UK. The striking, modern arrangements are cut and packed in Holland, then whisked across the Channel for next-day delivery.

Flowers Australia

http://www.australianflowers.net/

Flowers Australia is a Melbourne-based florist that delivers flowers – including Australian natives – locally, nationally and around the world.

Virtual cards

Blue Mountain

http://www.bluemountain.com/

If it's too late for flowers, send a card by email. Blue Mountain has animated, musical cards for all occasions and circumstances. You need to be a paid-up member to access all the designs.

Shockwave.com

http://www.shockwave.com/sw/musicphotos/

Shockwave.com's Music & Photos section has sophisticated animated cards and tools for creating cards and puzzles from your own photographs. You can then send your masterpiece to your friends.

Jacquie Lawson

http://www.jacquielawson.com/

Some of the nicest cards on the Internet, with music and sophisticated animation. Designs featuring Lawson's dog, Chudleigh, are especially nice for children. You'll need to pay a membership fee.

Cards.co.za

http://www.cards.co.za/

Cards.co.za is a South African site with a wide selection of attractive cards. It has designs for all the usual occasions, humorous cards, party invitations and plain cards for uncategorizable communications.

Miscellaneous

eBay

http://www.ebay.com/

eBay is an auction site that lets you unload your unwanted junk on to other Internet users. You can also purchase the treasures they've carelessly spurned, for whatever you think they're worth. It works like any other auction, although you don't have to worry about scratching your nose – simply make your offer, and if it's the top bid when the auction closes, you win. eBay has local sites for many countries, including the UK, Canada, Australia, New Zealand, Singapore and Hong Kong.

CompUSA.com

http://www.compusa.com/

This online computer store has everything from hardware and software to accessories, components and furniture. You can narrow down your search by brand, price or key features.

dabs.com

http://www.dabs.com/

dabs.com is a UK mail-order company turned Internet retailer that offers a huge range of computer hardware and software. You can browse by product type or manufacturer, or opt for speed and search for a specific product.

Crucial

http://www.crucial.com/

Crucial is a memory specialist that makes it easy to order memory upgrades for your computer, even if you're a technological ignoramus. Select your computer's manufacturer, and then your model, and it'll tell you what you can install.

Carphone Warehouse

http://www.carphonewarehouse.com/

UK blabbermouths can purchase mobile phones and accessories from the Carphone Warehouse. If you're one of the three people who don't yet have a mobile, the Encyclopaedia Mobilia will fill you in on technologies, tariffs and phones.

Jessops

http://www.jessops.com/

Capture the moment with a camera from Jessops. The UK's largest chain of photographic stores has an online branch that sells regular and digital cameras and camcorders, plus the whole range of accessories. You can also search the database of used equipment or upload your digital photos and get them printed.

iQ TOYS

http://www.iqtoys.co.nz/

iQ Toys is a New Zealand-based store that specializes in educational toys. You can browse by age, type or brand, making it easy to select something appropriate. It ships all over the world, although Australian customers get their own site.

Finance and banking

The Motley Fool

http://www.fool.com/

The Motley Fool provides accessible advice on financial matters, from credit cards and loans to investments and pensions. You can also set up an online portfolio and track your stocks. There are separate versions for the US and the UK so you don't get dollars mixed up with pounds.

Wells Fargo

http://www.wellsfargo.com/

Wells Fargo offers an online banking service that lets you check your accounts and pay bills from anywhere with Internet access. Unfortunately it can't send dollar bills down the line, so you'll still have to make the occasional trip to an ATM.

Smile

http://www.smile.co.uk/

Smile is an Internet-only bank set up by the UK's Co-operative Bank. It offers current accounts and credit cards, loans and online share dealing. And since the Co-operative Bank is committed to ethical investing, you should end up with something to smile about. It helps if you like pink, though.

E*TRADE

http://www.etrade.com/

E★TRADE offers online trading in the US, Canada, the UK, Australia and several other countries. As well as placing buy and sell orders, you can track stocks, get personal market updates, set up customized charts and access company profiles.

eChoice

https://www.echoice.com.au/

eChoice is an Australian mortgage-matching service that lets you enter your requirements over the Internet. A consultant then calls you up to discuss any issues and tell you about matching products. It also has fact sheets and calculators that help you make sense of the whole business.

Employment

Job-Hunt.Org

http://www.job-hunt.org/

Job-Hunt.Org catalogs career and job-hunting Web sites. It has advice on creating an online résumé, protecting your privacy and using the Internet to find a job, plus over 9,000 links to other sites. There's lots of good information here and it'll give you plenty to think about as you take the next step towards career nirvana.

Monster

http://www.monster.com/

Gigantic job-search network with sites for many countries. You can search for jobs on a one-off basis or set up an agent that runs searches periodically and emails you the results. You can also create an online résumé and use it to apply for jobs, although you should read the privacy policy carefully first.

Guardian Unlimited Jobs

http://jobs.guardian.co.uk/

The Guardian newspaper's Jobs site has details of all the jobs advertised in the paper, plus additional Internet-only adverts. Like the paper, it has special sections for education, media and society jobs. You can also browse by employer or sector or conduct detailed searches. Registered users are alerted to new jobs by email and can save job ads and searches and create online profiles and résumés.

Australian JobSearch

http://www.jobsearch.gov.au/

Australian JobSearch is a government-run site with a searchable database that includes jobs advertised in Job Network Services around the country, published in some national newspapers and/or entered by employers. It also has a résumé builder and information about Work for the Dole activities.

Travel

World Travel Guide

http://www.worldtravelguide.net/

World Travel Guide is a huge online factbook with travel information about every country in the world, from Afghanistan to Zimbabwe. Find out what documents you'll need and what kind of weather to expect, get contact details for tourism boards and consulates and read a wealth of background material. It also has city and airport guides.

Foreign & Commonwealth Office

http://www.fco.gov.uk/

Read the UK Foreign & Commonwealth Office's country-specific travel advisories to find out where you shouldn't go and what you shouldn't do. Once the It'll Never Happen to Me! section has convinced you otherwise, you can find information about documents, insurance, health, money and the perils of drugs and sex tourism.

Lonely Planet

http://www.lonelyplanet.com/

The attractively presented Web site of the Lonely Planet guidebook series has a world guide for independent travelers, discussion boards, links to

other travel sites and a travel ticker that summarizes current travel warnings.

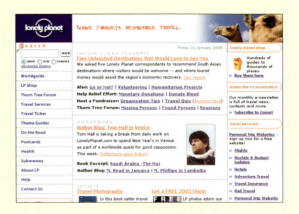

Rough Guides

http://www.roughguides.co.uk/

Rough Guides has a similar site with material from its guidebooks, discussion forums and space for registered members to create online journals.

Expedia

http://www.expedia.com/

Expedia is a travel-booking site with branches in several countries, including the US and UK. People from any country can use any Expedia site to make hotel and car reservations, but you can only purchase plane tickets from your own site. Enter your departure city, destination and dates, then click the Search button to find out what's available.

Travelocity

http://www.travelocity.com/

Travelocity is an alternative to Expedia with sites in the US, Canada, the UK and Germany. It pulls its flights from a different database, so it's worth checking both sites.

Visit Britain

http://www.visitbritain.com/

The British Tourist Authority has created a glossy sight that highlights the best that Britain has to offer. It customizes the site depending on where you're coming from, picking out appropriate attractions. You can also take a virtual tour through the landscapes, seasons, cities and regions.

Travel Canada

http://www.travelcanada.ca/

Study the possible destinations and experiences, then plan your trip with links to tour operators and travel agencies. Other features include an interactive map and a virtual tour.

Australia.com

http://www.australia.com/

Australia.com helps you plan your trip to the sixth largest country in the world. It has facts and figures, panoramic images and videos, advice on where to go, what to do and what to buy, and a calendar of major events. You can even compile the pages you like best into a personal travel brochure.

PureNZ

http://www.purenz.com/

PureNZ has features and facts to help you plan a trip to Kiwiland, plus travel journals in which New Zealanders recount expeditions to various parts of the country.

Visit Singapore

http://www.visitsingapore.com/

The Singapore Tourism Board's Visit Singapore site has lots of information about things to do in the Lion City. There's a list of 101 ways to live it up, with details of foods to try and places to hang out, and a directory of tours. Any pages that seem useful can be transferred to the Print Cart, which compiles them into a single document for easy printing.

Encounter South Africa

http://www.encounter.co.za/

South African Tourism's Web site explains why the country is unique: among other things, it's where you'll find "the world's oldest rocks, the world's oldest fossils, and the world's newest democracy". It has articles on the nature, history and people of South Africa, plus guides to the provinces.